TWISTED TECH

TWISTED TECH

The Death of Privacy
in the Digital Age

Adrienne,
thanks so much for your support!
can't wait to see what you do post ND.

Scott J McClallen

Scott McClallen

NEW DEGREE PRESS

TWISTED TECH
The Death of Privacy in the Digital Age

ISBN
978-1-63730-832-5   *Paperback*
978-1-63730-894-3   *Kindle Ebook*
978-1-63730-956-8   *Digital Ebook*

*To my late Grandma Mary, who planted a passion
for reading and knowledge in me at a young age, as
well as a healthy distrust of government.*

*Also to music and caffeine, which scared away the fear of
failure and pushed me to finish this book: a life goal.*

CONTENTS

———

INTRODUCTION:

———

"All human beings have three lives:
public, private, and secret."

—GABRIEL GARCÍA MÁRQUEZ

The internet is a double-edged sword, providing incredible services but at a high cost that isn't always monetary.

For Bilal Ahmed, the website PatientsLikeMe was a lifesaver. He could disclose his struggle with depression after the death of his mother to real-life humans who shared his pain and embarrassment without word spreading around his block in Sydney, Australia (Angwin 2015, 1,3.)

Across the world in Arkansas, Sharon Gill, a forty-two-year-old single mother, was attempting to get off antidepressants but didn't want her neighbors knowing (ibid.). The forum connected people who otherwise never would have met but struggled with medical conditions or habits for which they didn't want to be judged (ibid.). The relationship centered on privacy and no loose lips. In 2010, PatientsLikeMe noticed a user breaking in and scraping personal data and conversations for specific medical conditions so they could sell it (ibid.).

That culprit was the Nielsen Media-Research Company, selling the information to drug makers (ibid.). PatientsLikeMe sent a cease-and-desist letter but then admitted it's also been watching, scraping, and selling user data to pharmaceutical companies (ibid.).

Too often, people assume that social media brings us together. I wrote this book to explain the negative aspects of social media and included stories you can use to explain to those close to you why using tech responsibly matters.

In every industry, information is power —especially when it's usernames and passwords that unlock banks accounts, life investments, and Google Photos.

The internet created the ultimate invisible network that connects billions of people influenced by a handful of tech nerds. Those tech companies influence our lives through opaque algorithms that control what news we see, what statuses appear in what order, suggested friends, and now dating suggestions. Their workers decide what speech should be black-holed and who's allowed to share thoughts to the world via Facebook and Twitter.

Facebook has nearly three billion users (Gramlich 2021). How will these companies use this influence? To swing elections? To suppress government criticism during COVID-19 mass deaths in India?

Tech can be used for good or evil. The internet provides a scalable revenue model for widespread fraud and crime, taking advantage of those who are computer illiterate, careless, or inexperienced. In August of 2013, an unknown entity committed the largest known data breach in history, impacting all of Yahoo's three billion users (Perlroth 2017). As we continually post more online, companies and the government are grabbing as much data as possible—on your buying habits, political views, and how you spend your time.

Not only is the data you provide collected, but also even the data that friends and family share about you is collected to build social media companies' revenue models. Your data is sold whether you're a user or not. This means groups including law enforcement have access to personal information the police would otherwise need search warrants to get.

I'm compelled to write on this topic because the world as we know it is hurtling toward the complete death of privacy. Even local governments package and sell data (Klosowski 2021). And once we reach that point, there may be no return. In a world with a shrinking expectation of privacy, we must acknowledge what parts of our lives are private, public, and secret. The line between them is blurred, and if we want privacy and secrets, we must work harder than ever to keep them.

I wrote this book to sow a healthy dose of skepticism and cynicism into every reader's mind to question the seemingly all-powerful tech companies and how the government spends your tax dollars.

I've continued questioning power—to the chagrin of the majority of my teachers since kindergarten—leading to a litany of detentions for my ravenous curiosity for asking "why" and conveying strong skepticism that led to me majoring in economics and journalism and eventually landing journalism jobs where I get paid to ask hard questions to strangers.

This book encompasses the interviews, stories, and books I've read over the past ten years as a journalist that've led me to conclude that only you can take control of your life, choose how much information to divulge to the government, and to raise awareness about the vanishing boundaries separating our information that is public, private, and secret.

This book is wide-ranging because my pre-order readers range from sixty-six-year-olds who predated the internet to people born in the early 2000s who have never known the world without it. The latter mostly couldn't care less about privacy, while the former are skeptical of placing personal information on the internet. So, if a chapter bores you or doesn't apply, skip it. Life's too short to read boring books.

But no matter your age, this book is designed to raise questions: How much privacy am I willing to sacrifice for accessibility?

How much power am I willing to hand over to the government under the guise of safety? Initially, the Hong Kong government drastically stamped out COVID-19 cases at the cost of tracking every person and their phone, similarly to China's social credit system. Is the tradeoff worth it?

Either our kids or we must deal with the future of facial recognition and the internet that could distort an otherwise bright, free future into a nightmare like Black Mirror if we allow the decay of civil liberties via outbreak of government manipulation and control.

The internet is only thirty-two years old, a nascent industry compared to a 135-year history for cars (Romano 2019). We must ensure the internet is still a free, open, and blooming industry in one hundred years instead of weaponized by governments and tech companies.

This book targets a wide group of people—from those curious why targeted ads follow them around and how much data their phone shares about their habits, to those wondering if Facebook could swing a presidential election to attorneys who sue the government and tech companies into submission, to parents who worry their children will drunk-post a stupid comment on Facebook that will, fifteen years later, get them thrown out of medical school.

The base ingredient for readers is a driving hunger to be left alone and given privacy from those who want to abuse or sell your data. This could apply to children who want to teach their elderly parents about the danger of internet fraud, a frequent traveler who crosses the border and wants to know where the line stands between Transportation Security Administration patting you down for weapons and seizing your phone to download nude pictures of your wife.

I've read over thirty-four books on the idea of privacy, technology, and the history of power-hungry governments using it to abuse their power across the world written by Julie Angwin, Julian Assange, Bruce Schneier, and how tech titans like Mark Zuckerberg and Google's Eric Schmidt have accomplished incredible feats like connecting and mapping the whole world.

How much personal information are you willing to share with the world? Whom you swipe right on Tinder, your driving habits, or your credit card statements?

This book will explain where we stand with data privacy, why you should care, what you should worry about, how to talk to your mom/kids/friends about social media, and how you can maximize the benefits of social media while minimizing negative consequences like depression or needless comment battles that leave you angrily typing late into the night.

Our data is inherently who we are. How we spend time and money is an extension of our values, and in the age of big, cheap data, for the first time, we can collect ridiculous amounts of it.

Our digital data should carry the same protections as the Fourth Amendment to our physical items because now, we carry our most precious items in our metadata and behind passcodes or facial recognition—including health conditions, financial statements, wills, and more.

A common refrain to the rejection of mass surveillance is, "If you have nothing to hide, then you have nothing to fear."

This phrase fundamentally misunderstands the Unites States Justice system and the burden of proof, as well as blatant overcriminalization as yearly taxpayer expenditure climbs to new records.

If law enforcement needs to tap into your personal data, tell them to come back with a warrant.

PART 1

Welcome. In the next ten chapters, I'll introduce you to the wonders and nightmares of the internet. We'll talk about privacy in today's age, explain Section 230 and how it applies to companies moderating content, and past times the government has abused data. We'll wrap up this section discussing why some believe tech companies moderating content is "tyranny," frustrations of dealing with vague and secretive tech companies, and the dangers of growing up online where some mistakes are never forgotten.

CHAPTER 1

NOTHING TO HIDE, BUT EVERYTHING TO LOSE

——

"They who can give up essential liberty to obtain a little temporary safety deserve neither liberty nor safety."
—(BENJAMIN FRANKLIN 1779)

Knowing just my name, you can learn my address, the city I live in, where I work, and so much more just by Googling it and using the Freedom of Information Act. You can learn even more if you comb through ten pages of results on Google, such as whom I've talked to, and find many of the over 5,000 articles I've written.

If you're my Snapchat friend, you see a lot more—views from my apartment that clearly identify the building I live in, the struggles and triumphs of everyday life, and whom I spend time with. By the time I'm thirty-five, you can nearly know me just using my personal information placed on social media, this book, and more.

Granted, I placed my work history on LinkedIn. I allow strangers to find me easily online via privacy settings, and that's on purpose for whistleblowers and work opportunities, but it also means I get many friend requests from bots trying to steal my information.

In a world with a shrinking expectation of privacy, we must acknowledge what parts of our lives are private, public, and secret.

PUBLIC

Your life is public when walking in most downtowns, driving on an interstate with automatic license plate scanners if your car is registered with the state, or using "public" social media privacy settings like Instagram and Facebook. You have privacy inside your home, but that ends when you exit, including your trash that's public if left for collection.

PRIVATE

The shampoo you use to stop balding early. The late-night Snapchats you send to a group of close friends. What you buy with your credit card and how often you eat at Chipotle and In-N-Out.

This is like the "quiet enjoyment" clause of apartment leases or hotel rules. You're free to get drunk, have fun, and watch the Detroit Lions choke in the last fifteen minutes on Sunday as long as you don't get belligerent, bother your neighbors, and fight someone at the snack machine.

And in return, your landlord has limited access to your dwelling place. You won't fear waking up to a landlord waiting in your living room, asking for rent at 6 a.m. on the first day of the month. Your lease guarantees they won't search your apartment looking for the communal snack box taken from the lobby, or in other ways, abuse their power.

SECRET

Some things, we want to keep secret, like taking antidepressants, a malignant tumor, alcoholism, and whether you have a concealed carry permit. Except for the last item, those things are none of the government's business unless you tell them. Other than that, you have a right to be left alone. It's none of law enforcement's business if you attend Alcoholics Anonymous, whether you've had an abortion or if you called a suicide hotline two years ago after an incredibly rough day. Mass surveillance opens a door for weaponizing personal data for blackmail, criminal prosecution, or other threats.

Both parties love mass surveillance when they're in power, but John Gilmore, a founder of the Electronic Frontier Foundation, provides a good rule of thumb: "Never give a government a power you would not want a despot to have" (Granick p7). If you wouldn't trust former President Donald Trump with a certain power, don't give it to President Joe Biden either. Absolute power corrupts absolutely (Acton 1887).

The idea of privacy has been controversial since the 1800s. In an 1888 Henry James' novel, *The Reverberator* a king muses: "[I]f these people had done bad things they ought to be ashamed of themselves and he couldn't pity them, and if they hadn't done them there was no need of making such a rumpus about other people knowing."

This begs the question: what does privacy mean? We all waive our privacy when we appear in public near cameras, swipe our credit card, or even carry a cell phone.

It's worth noting that the word "privacy" doesn't appear in the Fourth Amendment. Instead of protecting a "right to privacy" the Amendment protects privacy by defining a "right to be secure" in property ("persons, houses, papers, and effects") against unreasonable intrusions, i.e., those not accompanied by a warrant or the need for emergency action.

Twenty-four hours a day, thousands of cameras around Detroit, at gas stations, restaurants, grocery and liquor stores, apartment buildings, churches, and schools, live-stream the daily lives of Detroiters into the Police Department's downtown head-quarters (Project Green Light website). And Motor City isn't alone. Many other cities rely on live-stream footage. Humans are routine-oriented, whether it's when and where we work, when we hit the gym, and/or who we see during the weekend.

Just because we waive our privacy rights in some capacity, does it mean we completely waive them? Are there exceptions? Most people register vehicles through a state entity, which means your license plate or other features can be used to identify you. If you're registered for Transportation Security Administration pre-check or have a concealed pistol permit, then multiple intelligence agencies have your fingerprints. Also, anyone who travels in a US airport agrees to be sur-veilled through facial recognition.

Is public footage of us evidence of wrongdoing? Should we stop caring and hole up in our homes for the rest of our lives?

Edward Snowden explained in a Reddit "Ask Me Anything" forum in 2015, "Arguing that you don't care about the right to privacy because you have nothing to hide is no different than saying you don't care about free speech because you have nothing to say. A free press benefits more than just those who read the paper."

Later at a New Yorker Festival in a remote interview, he explained further. "When you say, 'I have nothing to hide,' you're saying, 'I don't care about this right.' You're saying, 'I don't have this right, because I've got to the point where I have to justify it.' The way rights work is the government has to justify its intrusion into your rights" (Ha 2014).

In other words, just because you don't care if an FBI agent is reading your text message fight with your wife about an affair doesn't mean you still won't care when someone blackmails your campaign for public office with years-old text messages. Supporters of all-encompassing surveillance argue innocent people should have nothing to fear about government recording the public. It's only criminals that should be concerned. This is a short-sighted view. We all have parts of our life that are private, public, and secret. An abortion you had ten years ago, the Alcoholics Anonymous group you attend, or an arrest when you were a minor for a now-expunged conviction likely land in the "secret" category.

In Friedrich Dürrenmatt's 1960's novel *Traps*, retired lawyers place a man on trial, and the man inquires what his crime shall be. "'An altogether minor matter,' the prosecutor replied. 'A crime can always be found.'" (in 213 Notes to pages 24–43).

Do you mind if a stranger or law enforcement officer listens to your conversations with friends?

"The main problem with the "nothing to hide" argument is assuming that privacy is important only if you have something to hide," Ignacio Cofone, a New York University research fellow and privacy expert told Mic. "Privacy is portrayed, then, as something for deviants. If we start arguing how everyone has something to hide, then we've already lost" (Harding 2018).

Privacy journalist Kashmir Hill explained in finding awkward instances of the "Friends You May Know" section of Facebook: "A one-night stand from 2008, a person you got a couch from on Craigslist in 2010, a landlord from 2013. If they ever put you in their phone, or you put them in yours, Facebook could log the connection if either party were to upload their contacts," Hill wrote (Vaidhyanathan 2018, 61).

We have thousands of connections that seem inconsequential until they aren't, like when someone you sold a couch to was convicted on child sex trafficking charges, and authorities want to know if the couch was the only thing you sold them.

"That accumulation of contact data from hundreds of people means that Facebook probably knows every address you've lived at, every email address you've used, every landline and cell phone number you've been associated with, all of your nicknames, any social network profiles associated with you, all your former instant message accounts, and anything else someone might have added about you to their phone book," Hill wrote (ibid.).

Journalist Glenn Greenwald explains in a TED Talk that even tech executives value their privacy, although they claim otherwise. Ex-Google CEO Eric Schmidt told his employees to stop talking to journalists after CNET published Schmidt's information gained solely through Google. (Greenwald 2014 3:07).

In a talk, Schmidt responded to a journalist saying, "If you have something that you don't want anyone to know, maybe you shouldn't be doing it in the first place" (ibid. 2:21). Facebook's Mark Zuckerberg bought the four surrounding houses around his thirty-million-dollar home but says that we don't have an expectation of privacy (Riggs 2013). Rules for thee, but not me?

In 2012, *The Wall Street Journal* reported that an LGBTQ chorus accidentally outed the surprise sexuality of two gay students at the University of Texas at Austin by adding them to a public Facebook group (Fowler 2012). The move outed their surprise sexuality to almost 200 people, including an unsupportive father (ibid.). That night, twenty-two-year-old Bobbi Duncan's father left vitriolic messages on her phone, demanding she renounce same-sex relationships, threatening to sever family ties (ibid.). Duncan said she cried all night on a friend's couch. "I felt like someone had hit me in the stomach with a bat." The president didn't know the software would automatically notify Facebook friends, *The Wall Street Journal* reported (ibid.).

Social platforms outing your personal information to hundreds is bad enough, but at least Facebook can't throw you in jail or arrest you. However, the government can, and it's collecting much of the same information. This could get even worse with overzealous prosecutors and police who abuse surveillance as a method to fish for victimless crimes—a larger problem of overcriminalization. There are 27,000 pages of federal statutes—even sharing a Netflix password is a federal crime (Williams 2016) (Rosenweig 2003). Even if you're an upstanding citizen, you're likely breaking some obscure law.

In *American Spies: Modern Surveillance, Why You Should Care, and What To Do About It,* Jennifer Stisa Granick points out this flawed logic: "One in four people in the United States has a criminal record," she writes. "This information is used to deny access to public benefits, housing, jobs and professional licensing. But something closer to 100 percent of Americans have committed crimes other than mere driving infractions. We just haven't been caught.... Consider how very different your life could have been had you been caught and convicted for things you have done" (Granick 2017, 128).

US circuit judge Alex Kozinski makes a similar point in his article, "You're (Probably) a Federal Criminal." Most Americans are criminals, but don't know it, he writes. For example: If you bring a shot of alcohol on a plane and drink it without the flight attendant serving it to you because you don't want to pay ten dollars for a mediocre drink, congratulations. You're now a federal criminal. (Electronic Code of Federal Regulations) Indiana bans the coloring of birds and rabbits; Massachusetts can punish those who frighten pigeons from their nests. Federal regulation prohibits exporting pennies or nickels out of the United States without a license, Mike Chase writes in "How to Become a Federal Criminal." Thankfully, these rules aren't enforced often. But selective enforcement of laws opens a door for abuse. The age-old saying, "Ignorance of the law is no excuse" to dodge liability no longer holds because of blatant overcriminalization.

The Manhattan Institute and the Mackinac Center for Public Policy released a study, "Overcriminalizing the Wolverine State: A Primer and Possible Reforms for Michigan." The report found Michigan had at least 3,102 statutory crimes, and that most of them lay outside the state's criminal code (ibid.). It also showed that more than 26 percent of the felonies and more than 59 percent of the misdemeanors did not explicitly require the state to make a showing of criminal intent (*mens rea*) on the part of the accused (ibid.). Don't believe me? Follow @Crimeaday on Twitter. On Oct. 23, 2020: "USC §5687 & 27 CFR §31.202(a) make it a federal crime to possess a liquor bottle that has been refilled with liquor since it was originally filled (Crimeaday 2020). So, when I dumped five or six shots out of a handle of Everclear into a vodka bottle so it would fit on my hard alcohol shelf, I became a federal criminal.

Everybody has something to hide. You just need to look hard enough.

In a related argument, Judge Richard Posner contends, "[W]hen people today decry lack of privacy, what they want, I think, is mainly something quite different from seclusion: they want more power to conceal information about themselves that others might use to their disadvantage" (Solove 2007). Privacy involves a person's "right to conceal discreditable facts about himself" (ibid.).

Daniel Woislaw, an attorney at the libertarian Pacific Legal Foundation said the "nothing to hide" argument fundamentally confuses America's founding principles. "Not having anything to hide isn't relevant to whether you can exclude the government from your property," Woislaw said. "One of the fundamental principles of property law and property itself is the right to exclude others from your property." The right of exclusion from private property is widespread in the South where they'll be left alone, described colorfully by the "Trespassers will be shot. Survivors will be shot again" signs.

It applies to the Fourth Amendment as well. "Just like your neighbor can't waltz into your house without your consent or without some sort of court permission, saying that he can—because he knows you stole an item from him, or something of that nature—the government also can't trespass on your private property. I don't think any of us care to live in a world where the government can enter your property for whatever reason it wants, whenever it wants, just because you shouldn't expect to have privacy if you don't have anything to hide."

"I can't imagine anybody who forwards that argument would care to live in a world where that was the case," Woislaw said.

Privacy and the Fourth Amendment are similar. As my doormat says, "Get a warrant." We have the right to live without government interference. Every person holds the presumption of innocence.

"So it's not up to us to prove that we have nothing to hide from the government. It's up to the government to prove that we do have something to hide," Woislaw said. "And then to go through the proper processes that respects due process of law and property rights and privacy rights to prove it. And then to take us to court and then to prove it there. So, it sort of inverts the whole idea of American justice, which presumes innocence until guilt is proven when the government claims the power to search our property without a warrant and then claim that only a criminal would oppose that power."

The "nothing to hide" idea also violates the separation of powers between the judicial and executive branches, and due process because judges are meant to check the power of law enforcement. When you stand in court in front of a judge, it's not you versus the team of law enforcement and the judge. The judge is a neutral third party.

"The judges and the courts keep these officers accountable by making sure that when they go in when they intrude on some of the places of most fundamental freedom and protection— which is, of course, the house and our personal papers and our effects—they have a warrant and have followed a proper process," Woislaw said.

Ultimately, while people may not be worried about most of their life being exposed, we all have skeletons in our closets. Through technology, it has become easier and easier to collect, uncover, and disseminate this information. We must take precautions to safeguard our own privacy and be aware others would use our inner/private lives against us.

CHAPTER 2

WHO RULES THE INTERNET?

———

When Senator Ron Wyden (D-OR) and Representative Chris Cox (R-CA) wrote Section 230 of the Communications Decency Act of 1996, which provides civil liability immunity to online platforms' third-party content such as comments, only about twenty million people in America were internet users (Farhad 2009). Pre-internet, document distribution services only provided one-way communication. Now 4.6 billion people—or 59 percent of the global population—are two-way active internet users (Johnson 2021). More people are connected online than ever before, and it's causing toxic comment sections to alleged misinformation to overloaded servers for some social media companies.

It's hard to overestimate the importance of internet policy that affects over 310 million Americans, assuming roughly eighteen million people don't use the internet (Morris 2021). If internet policy didn't protect nascent online industries, they likely would have been sued into the ground, taking with them profit, jobs, and tax revenue.

Section 230 is core to the structure of the entire internet, from Facebook to Etsy to YouTube to Reddit to Eventbrite. However, Section 230 doesn't protect against some online crimes, such as intellectual property theft for selling fake LEGOs on Etsy or sharing child porn (Masnick 2020). But if the rules let companies run wild, stealing, sabotaging, and abusing their power to restrict competition, that would also choke growth.

The context of Section 230 is people talking shit about each other and subsequently suing. In the 1990s, an online newsletter called Rumorville accused rival Scuttlebutt of being a "scam" (Fitzgerald 2018). Skuttlebutt sued CompuServe, Rumorville's online service provider for publishing false damaging statements. The judge ruled CompuServe wasn't liable for distributed content (ibid.).

But on the same topic, a court later ruled the opposite even though the speech might have been accurate. In the 1990s, Jordan Belfort's brokerage firm Stratton Oakman defrauded customers and sparked the idea behind the film *The Wolf of Wall Street* (ibid.). However, when an anonymous user called the brokerage firm a "cult of brokers who either lie for a living or get fired," the firm sued the online service provider Prodigy, which prided itself as a "family-friendly" company and tried to take down porn or vile, gross, offensive content, and won because the online service provider moderated content (Lee 2020) (Fitzgerald 2018). Prodigy was deemed liable because they attempted to keep obscene items—possibly porn, defamation, and worse—from their consumers (ibid.).

Several lawmakers believed the case law resulted in perverted incentives for online publishers. Section 230 was originally titled "Internet Freedom and Family Empower-ment Act of 1996" and aimed to ensure investors wouldn't drop tech companies because legal loopholes allowed them to be sued into oblivion because one person posted libel, mean messages, and sometimes, the truth. But at the same time, the law intended to ensure kids talking in chat rooms didn't see porn, beheadings, and a wide range of other ter-rible things on the internet.

Carl Szabo is the vice president and general counsel of NetChoice, a tech policy company whose customers include Google, Facebook, Airbnb, Lyft, and PayPal, according to its website. He argues Section 230 empowers tech titans to build platforms that employ millions of people and serve even more.

"The entire design of Section 230 was to empower platforms to engage in the content moderation that they find to be appropriate," he told me in a phone interview.

Szabo argues the internet was the Wild West before Section 230. Platforms couldn't remove pornography, religious groups couldn't remove atheists, and atheist groups couldn't remove religious people. I think most people understand why this is a problem. Can you imagine if companies like Facebook or Twitter couldn't remove posts and ban users who are trolls?

He describes Section 230 as the Good Samaritan Law. "If you had done absolutely nothing, you'd have zero liability," Szabo said. "If you find someone not breathing on the side of the road, and you give them CPR and in the process of doing so, you happen to break their ribs, they're not able to sue you because we have Good Samaritan Laws that prevent liability in an effort to encourage people to do the right thing and not be afraid of being sued."

If we give tech companies too much liability, then angry users would sue them into the ground. If we gave them no liability, they have no reason to enforce their rules and remove bad content.

Many people I've spoken to on both political spectrums have advocated for reforming Section 230, but Szabo argued that would hurt free speech and wouldn't necessarily stop content moderation. If you eliminate Section 230, you still have to adhere to the community standards and the terms of service agreement. The contract that rules our social media use can still moderate content if they choose. "If you want to increase free speech, Section 230 does exactly that because it enables content moderation," Szabo said, adding that a dystopian all-content-goes would be a world no one wants to live in, which would result in fewer people using social media services.

Companies respond to incentives, so if Section 230 was revoked, Facebook might take down anything that could risk their liability protection. They might move to a verification system where you have to prove your posts meet some threshold of non-controversy before you can post at will, or just delay publishing of your tweet or post until it could be reviewed by a moderator, which could take a very long time depending on the number of posts and moderators.

Without Section 230, as you increase content moderation, you increase legal liability. So, there's actually a perverse incentive for content moderation to censor users and advertisers because the companies want to dodge lawsuits. For example, if I called for violence against another person via Facebook, Facebook could be sued. Now imagine that problem on a nationwide scale. I don't see how many online tech companies could survive.

Robby Soave is an editor at Reason who covers free speech, is the author of *Tech Panic: Why We Shouldn't Fear Facebook and the Future*, and was named on the 2016 *Forbes* 30 Under 30 for Law and Policy.

"If you think they're biased against conservatives, this might actually inflame these biases as they become even more cautious about some edgy, right-wing speech," Soave said." This just seems like a really bad idea."

Many conservatives say revoking Section 230 would spark a firestorm of free speech, but it's not that simple. Soave says the biggest mistake people, particularly Republicans make about Section 230 is you have to be a platform or a publisher. If a social media site moderates content, then it's a publisher rather than a platform, so it should be subjected to the same sort of legal regimen or liability as a traditional publisher, like *Reason Magazine* or Simon and Schuster.

"That's completely wrong," Soave said. "What Section 230 does is simply state that social media companies are not to be considered the publisher of the speech that appears on the platform. Facebook, the company, is not the author of my posts on Facebook. So, you could sue me if I wrote something on Facebook that was libelous, but you couldn't sue Facebook."

"The second part says that that designation doesn't get taken away from the social media company, even if it engages in moderation. So even if Facebook makes decisions that are like a traditional publisher. They say we're going to take down this content, but we're going to leave up this content. Even if they do that, they're still entitled to the full protections of Section 230."

If you think about it, the publisher shouldn't be liable for a dispute between two of its users. Facebook has nearly three billion monthly users, and even a company as big as Facebook can't monitor that many posts.

The R Street Institute's Shoshanna Weismann explains the struggle of monitoring the content of billions of users.

"Facebook has billions of users, and Twitter has hundreds of millions. Last year, Facebook released a report showing the billions of pieces of content it moderated, from child exploitation to terrorist propaganda," she wrote. "It would be literally impossible for any amount of human moderators to see every piece of content posted. That each website should be liable for content they did not create or even see is ridiculous" (Statista 2021) (Twitter 2021) (Weissmann 2020).

THE ENEMY OF MY ENEMY IS MY FRIEND?

The Left and Right are both mad at Big Tech, but the former demands they do more content moderation while the latter demands they do less. Former President Donald Trump, who's leading a class-action lawsuit against Big Tech companies, alleges that Big Tech companies are being used "to impose illegal and unconstitutional government censorship" (Trump 2021).

Trump says Big Tech and government are "actively coordinating to remove content from the platforms" led by the Centers for Disease Control and Prevention that is using the government to control online speech (ibid.). In effect, Big Tech has been illegally deputized as the censorship arm of the US government. This should alarm you no matter your political persuasion" (ibid.).

This matters because there's a stark difference between a private company censoring you, which they can do, and the government censoring you through private companies.

Unfortunately, there isn't great data to show whether social media giants discriminate against political persuasions. But overall, Facebook's top-performing sites are overwhelmingly conservative, likely because it's geared to older users, according to the *New York Times*'s tech writer Kevin Roose.

On July 20, 2020, Facebook's head of news feed John Hegeman told Roose that Facebook subsidiary Crowdtangle, which tracks story popularity, doesn't tell the full story since it only ranks posts by "engagement" or the number of times users like, comment, or share the post. Hegeman said that posts "reach"–how many people see a post—is a better metric.

Hegeman shared links with the widest reach on Facebook, compared to posts with the highest engagement on the same day. On July 5, the posts with the highest engagement came from Franklin Graham, Ben Shapiro, *Breitbart*, *ForAmerica*, and *CNN*. By contrast, the links with the widest reach that day came from *The Los Angeles Times, MSNBC, Ranker, BuzzFeed*, and *ABC News* (Holmes 2020).

NewsWhip, an independent social analytics firm, publishes its own monthly lists of top Facebook publishers and articles. NewsWhip ranks by engagement rather than reach and includes both conservative outlets such as *Daily Wire, Breitbart, Fox News* and *CNN* and the *Mail Online* and *New York Post* (Nicholson 2020).

Parler, a relatively new social media company touted itself as a bastion for free speech—except Parler didn't know what it was doing. Pro-tip: If you're going to act like a free-market champion independent from existing behemoths, don't use Amazon as your web host. Despite claiming to champion free speech, Parler blocks people it finds annoying, essentially blocking what many think is "free speech" (Masnick 2020).

But that isn't a bad thing. Private companies can ban annoying people and creeps, but they should have clear standards for blocking people and applied equally.

In its 2019 transparency report, Facebook says it removed 11.6 million pieces of content deemed child nudity and sexual exploitation of children in the third quarter—double the number removed in that category for the first quarter (Facebook 2019). Some argue the sexual exploitation of children wouldn't happen on the internet if the government forced residents to link online activity with their state ID. Although well-intentioned, Szabo warned against terrible ramifications.

First off, we currently have systems based around our names and identities, like Facebook and LinkedIn, and that doesn't stop us from attacking, hitting on, and annoying each other online. Section 230 doesn't enable hate speech on the internet; the First Amendment does.

"People can be jerks in real-life to your face," Szabo said. "The idea doesn't match reality. It's a nice dream that we'd all be civil to each other, but civility between people didn't always last before the internet, and it isn't going to come back just because we have real-name systems.

But the worst issue is that it undermines and misses the value of anonymity in our society.

"We have organizations that are built entirely around the notion of anonymity," Szabo said. "One example is literally called Alcoholics Anonymous." There are many benefits to anonymity—the priest-penitent privilege, whistleblowers, and particularly vulnerable people.

"You don't necessarily need anonymity if you're going to say a very safe thing," Szabo said. "If you're going to say something that never challenges authority or questions the collective norm, anonymity isn't really necessary because society will defend you. It is for those who are going to raise issues and concerns, that need the sometimes protection of anonymity."

Courts have previously ruled in favor of anonymity.

In 1958, The Supreme Court ruled the National Association for the Advancement of Colored People (NAACP) didn't have to disclose to the state of Alabama its list of rank-and-file members. In other words, the First Amendment freedom of association includes the association to anonymity. And in that case, there's anonymity of donations.

"Now we're talking about anonymity of who you are," Szabo said. "And the idea of having 'papers, please' for the internet is a very scary thought, however well-intentioned it is."

"And then Section 230 came along and allowed platforms to decide what's best for their users and advertisers. If you want to be a site with no pornography, you can do it. If you want to be a site with pornography, you can do that too."

"I'm hoping that lawmakers understand the amazing balance of the most good with the least harm, which is Section 230, they don't try to undo this fundamental law that empowers so much."

"All proposals to revise have the same problem," Soave said. "If you revise Section 230 to allow publishers to moderate but can't be politically biased, what does that mean? Who's going to enforce that? And eventually, you will run up against that problem that in some ways, section 230 is just making more obvious and more direct what the First Amendment says."

Texas Senator Ted Cruz, who has a law degree from Harvard, believes Section 230 requires neutral platforms (Padhi 2018). During a 2018 hearing, Cruz cut straight to the point and asked Zuckerberg, "The predicate for Section 230 immunity under the [Communications Decency Act] is that you're a neutral public forum. Do you consider yourself a neutral public forum, or are you engaged in political speech, which is your right under the First Amendment?" (ibid.). "Are you a

First Amendment speaker expressing your views, or are you a neutral public forum allowing everyone to speak?" (ibid.).

To legislate such a "neutrality" requirement for online platforms—besides being unworkable—would be unconstitutional under the First Amendment. The First Amendment only protects the government from censoring your speech, which is a good thing. I welcome anyone to attempt to police a platform for political neutrality. It sounds good in theory, but it's impossible. Who makes the rules? Who deems if a post is neutral? Who polices it? What about their own biases?

It's easy to find trash takes on reforming Section 230 or other laws and agencies of people who want to weaponize it to choke out competition via government power. Writer Max Boot might take home the award for the worst take. On January 18, 2021, Boot tweeted, "Biden needs to reinvigorate the FCC to slow the lies and sedition from Fox and other right-wing broadcasters. Or else the terrorism we saw on Jan. 6 may be only the beginning, rather than the end, of the plot against America." Again, the First Amendment protects against government censoring free speech—exactly what Boot is arguing for.

Thankfully, in a free and open forum, logic and humor prevail. Ari Cohn, a First Amendment Lawyer and counsel for TechFreedom, responded with a comment garnering more than a thousand likes: "This wasn't a particularly well thought-out tweet, I have to say." "That sounds scary and fascistic," *Washington Examiner* writer Tim Carney commented.

"Handing the power over to the government is easily one of the most dangerous ideas that you can have, with respect to the First Amendment," Szabo said in response when asked about Boot's tweet. "The fundamental purpose of the First Amendment actually mirrors the fundamental purpose of Section 230. That is to increase free speech."

This idea of regulating platforms as neutral is similar to enacting "neutral fact-checkers" who, in reality, just flag everything against their own political ideology. It's a joke. Cruz and other lawmakers push government—or central planning—as a solution, except this violates the First Amendment, not to mention the majority of Congress have no idea how these platforms work.

If you need an example, watch one of the congressional hearings in which Mark Zuckerberg attempts to explain the internet and Facebook to Congress, most of whom were born pre-internet and have no idea how it runs.

"If [a version of Facebook will always be free], how do you sustain a business model in which users don't pay for your service?" Senator Orrin Hatch, an eighty-four-year-old Republican from Utah, asked in the hearing (Stewart 2018).

"Senator, we run ads," Zuckerberg responded (ibid.).

Congress has no authority to regulate speech online speech other than current laws against child porn and others. That's where the First Amendment applies since it's the government censoring a private company.

"Congress's attempt at making this benefit of 230 contingent on private companies adopting some congressionally mandated practices relating to speech, is going to have First Amendment problems, no matter how well-intended or structured it is, because the Supreme Court really doesn't like the government telling people what they can and cannot say," Soave said.

The internet is extremely complex and has advanced far past when the rules ruling it were made. There's no clear-cut ruler. Instead, it's run by old rules that some of Congress wants to update. Despite complaints from the left and right, if we feel that a specific tech company like Facebook or Twitter is unfairly censoring us, we can leave and find another platform or just ditch social media altogether. No matter what, we have to keep the internet a fair and free place instead of using it to favor the elite.

CHAPTER 3

HATE CRIMES?

———

Former commerce secretary Norman Mineta was eleven years old living in San Jose when the government sent his family to an internment camp in Heart Mountain, Wyoming, suspecting without evidence they were Japanese spies (Aratani 2018).

The crime? His family was Japanese Americans. And on March 29, 1942, several state governments forced evacuation and detention of Mineta and 120,000 other Japanese Americans, hauling them across the country like cattle with just a forty-eight-hour notice, according to the National Archives (ibid.).

All of this was because the families accurately answered the 1940 US Census, handing over their race, names, and addresses, only for the Census Bureau to snitch on them based only on race—one of the darkest violations of constitutional rights in American history (Minkel 2007). The states temporarily repealed the protection of Census data and imprisoned Japanese Americans in Arkansas, Arizona, California, Colorado, Idaho, Utah, and Wyoming (ibid.). People were right to be scared. Salem Media estimates about fifty-six million people died during the First World War and by the end, some nations seized more power or ceased to exist. But there's no excuse for imprisoning people because of their race.

The US government used that fear as an excuse to spy on their own people and do terrible things. The government has always pushed for completing the US Census as an act of patriotism to get the maximum amount of federal funding for your community spent to repair roads, fund hospitals, and health and human services safety nets for vulnerable families—but abused private data for terrible means. With the government collecting more and more data, there will be more excuses to abuse it and spy on us. In her book *Army Surveillance in America*, historian Joan M. Jensen notes of the World War I program, "What began as a system to protect the government from enemy agents became a vast surveillance system to watch civilians who violated no law but who objected to wartime policies or to the war itself." This has happened before.

The War Department relied on a volunteer organization, the American Protective League (APL) who agreed to report fellow citizens. The War Department would mark someone as a person of interest,—a malleable definition—signaling the APL to investigate (Gene 2003). The APL racked up nearly a quarter of a million members investigating six million incidents by the end of the war (ibid.). The program resulted in catching one German spy (ibid.). Was the cost of six million investigations to catch one person worth shattering Americans' trust in their government, one that claims to be founded upon the freedom of speech, expression, and faith?

Freedom of speech means the government must respect speech, even when it's criticism. It's ironic that Martin Luther

King, Jr. Day is a federal holiday because former President George W. Bush's administration operated COINTELPRO, a 1960s-era federal surveillance program on more than one million Americans including "subversives," such as Rev. Martin Luther King, Jr., hippies opposed to the Vietnam war, and other nonviolent political groups that resulted in blackmailing King, suggesting he commit suicide instead of leading the Civil Rights Movement, according to Stanford University's research.

The FBI sent Martin Luther King, Jr., a recording of his non-marital sexcapades with the goal to get him to divorce his wife and threatened to release it to the public unless King committed suicide (ibid.).

During the Vietnam War, J. Edgar Hoover requested "complete surveillance of all Quakers" on suspicion they were sending food to Asia, and the FBI collected roughly 30,000 pages on alleged homosexuals who worked in government (ibid.).

The problem isn't isolated to the United States.

During the Holocaust, at least five European counties used population data to round up Jews for extermination. Governments for decades in the Soviet Union, East Germany, Argentina, China, Cuba, and others have been spying on their residents (ibid.).

For decades, the United States government has used the threat of terrorism to scare Americans into surrendering civil liberties. But the balance of security and privacy careens toward security during crises. America's privacy and security drastically lurched toward security the year planes crashed into the World Trade Centers in 2001. President Bush declared a War on Terror, but it might as well have been a war on personal privacy, secretly giving the NSA authority to spy on American citizens without a warrant, James Risen and Eric Lichtblau wrote in the *New York Times*.

Exactly forty-five days after 9/11, the lawmakers approved the ironically named the Patriot Act, which emboldened the government to enact mass surveillance on its own citizens, monitoring phone and email communications, banking records, and internet activity.

The Patriot Act opened a floodgate of legally dubious warrantless searches via "National Security Letters" (NSL) issued by FBI agents without a judge's approval to obtain people's phones, computer records, and credit and banking history, the ACLU explains. Between 2003 and 2006, The FBI issued 192,499 NSLs, but they only led to one terror-related conviction (ibid.).

"Although the power was intended to be used to prevent terror-related crimes, 76 percent of the sneak and peeks in 2010 were drug-related (ibid.). Law enforcement abused the loopholes to infringe on civil liberties because they either knew a judge otherwise wouldn't issue a search warrant, or they just didn't feel like going through the proper channels (ibid.). Less than one percent of sneak and peeks in 2010 were related to terrorist crimes (ibid.). The ACLU explains in a Q&A about the Pentagon's "Total Information Awareness Project" that its goal is to create an "ultra-large-scale" government database to try to identify terrorists.

Given the motto "Information is Power," the program displayed why the government can't be trusted with such wide-ranging power. A 2001 investigation by the *Detroit Free Press*'s M.L. Elrick found that over five years, more than ninety Michigan police officers, security guards, and dispatchers accessed the Law Enforcement Information Network (LEIN) database to help their friends or themselves stalk women, threaten motorists, track estranged spouses, and intimidate political opponents.

Who watches the watchman?

The Senate Judiciary Committee noted that "comments about the financial affairs, sex lives, and psychiatric histories of persons unaffiliated with the armed forces appear throughout the various records systems." Justice William O. Douglas denounced the practice, calling army surveillance "a cancer in our body politic." In other words, since the government has access to that personal and secret information, they will abuse it.

The government's problem is that it says it'll solve problems it can't—poverty, homelessness, drug addictions, student loan debt, and terror. The government wasn't created to fix every problem: that's what the private and nonprofit sectors do.

I'd run for cover and hide my wallet whenever the government declares war on something because it'll only augment the problem—whether that's in Afghanistan the "affordable college" conundrum or mortgage brokers. For example: the War on Terror.

Terrorism is a frightening concept because no amount of government interference can stop it. One person can build a bomb made with untraceable materials bought at Lowe's and blow the shit out of a subway, and there's nothing the NSA can do about it.

But the video of planes crashing through the World Trade Centers on September 11, 2001 is imprinted onto the minds of entire generations. At six years old, I remember watching news clips replaying the video for days, trying to understand what was happening.

It's human nature to turn to the government for help. When people are scared or chaos abounds, we want to do something, even if that action doesn't help the problem. So, after 9/11, the TSA banned liquids over 3.4 ounces, meaning we can't carry most drinks onto planes now. Does that really make us safer, or just thirsty?

Most surveillance systems are extremely inefficient to stop terrorism, Jennifer Granick, the surveillance and cybersecurity counsel with the ACLU Speech, Privacy, and Technology Project, explains in her book *American Spies: Modern Surveillance, Why You Should Care, and What to Do About It.*

"Pattern matching will never be very accurate at finding rare events," she wrote. "To identify a pattern, you have to have commonalities. But what commonalities do we see in terror attacks? Terrorism is rare and distinctive. The Oklahoma City bombing was not like the 1993 World Trade Center bombing, which was different from September 11, which was nothing like the Boston Marathon bombing. We can't look to the past to identify any common thing or things to look for" (Granick 2017, p. 91).

We fear terrorism because no matter how rare it is, there is no controlling it. But how much freedom are we willing to surrender under the guise of safety? A quick look into Australia shows how little freedom ruins life.

During the COVID-19 pandemic, South Australia forced residents to download an app that uses facial recognition and geolocation to prove they are adhering to a fourteen-day quarantine for travel within the country. They aren't allowed to leave the country, except under special permission from the government (O'Neil 2021). The app contacts people randomly who must prove their location within fifteen minutes (ibid.). This isn't the role of government. As long we pay taxes, the government should leave us alone.

RISKY BUSINESS?

We feel as if we won't die in a car crash if we drive the speed limit and wear our seatbelt.

A December 2015 poll showed 47 percent of respondents said they were worried a family member would be a victim of a terror attack (Granick 2017, p. 67). However, as Granick points out, more Americans are more likely to be crushed by furniture than be killed by a terrorist (ibid.). Moreover, "More died from gun violence in the United States in 2015 (13,400) than have died in over forty-five years from terrorism across Western Europe (6,411; 1970–2016)," Granick wrote (ibid.).

Matthew Guariglia, a policy analyst at the Electronic Frontier Foundation, argues that too much surveillance makes us less free and safe. For example, after terrorist attacks in Boston,

Orlando, and Manchester, authorities said they "were aware" of the perpetrator months or even years before. But they still didn't stop them (Miller 2013) (Dodd and Asthana 2017).

One reason is that the government believes they have to "collect it all"—even information about innocent people, which clogs the system when trying to sift through data to identify terrorists.

In Dark Mirror, journalist Barton Gellman's account of the Snowden leaks, CIA Chief Technical Officer compared dots to people's personal information. He argues we don't know the future value of a dot today, and we can't connect dots we don't have, so we must collect it all. That's possible today, a divergence from past human history thanks to miraculous advances in technology.

"It is nearly within our grasp to compute all human generated information," he wrote.

But this idea ignores the sheer amount of data people produce that's not relevant, which can distract from the actual terrorist's information. Too many irrelevant data points conflate the few terrorists' information.

"An intelligence system that is overextended is also ineffective and dangerous," Guariglia explains in a *Washington Post* op-ed. "NSA-contractor-turned-whistleblower Edward Snowden argued, 'We're monitoring everybody's communications, instead of suspects' communications. That lack of focus has caused us to miss leads that we should've had.' Snowden pointed to Boston bomber Tamerlan Tsarnaev, saying, 'If we hadn't spent so much on mass surveillance, if we had followed the traditional models, we might've caught him.'"

Guariglia said that machine learning and AI couldn't analyze data as well as humans, and right now, law enforcement agencies just have too much on their plate.

"The more information the government collects, the harder it becomes to make all that information useful and usable because it takes manpower, it takes analysis. To some extent, some places have tried to shoulder the burden of analysis of all that information onto machine learning and AI algorithms, which are notoriously often inaccurate. There's a lot of things about nuance that they don't understand."

BUT HOW DOES SURVEILLANCE HARM US?

"On a philosophical level, there is an erosion of the presumption of innocence," Guariglia said. "That when every single person in the United States or millions of people, or people are under surveillance one way or another, that it is a definitive sign from the government that they don't trust you."

While surveillance can gift clues such as license plate numbers, perpetrator's outfits, and numbers, many cameras film over pre-existing footage to the point that it diminishes the video's quality—security can harm innocent people.

"When a robbery happens, and there's grainy security camera footage and they run that against the facial recognition algorithm that it's trying to match it to; for instance, every driver's license owner in the state of Texas," Guariglia said.

"What the government is essentially saying is that each and every one of you could potentially be this suspect, and to see if you are, we are going to search your face."

But surveillance also leads to overcriminalization, and heavy surveillance is disproportionately in large, urban cities, Guariglia said.

"If you put any community under a microscope, under constant police surveillance, they will eventually find reasons to arrest people. There's a deep connection between where the majority of arrests are in America and how much surveillance there is on that place. If you took a suburban where there are almost no arrests, almost no crime, and you put it under the same level of scrutiny and surveillance that say, a city is under, you're going to start arresting people for jaywalking, drinking in public—for all sorts of stuff."

Mass surveillance data collection also tempts governments to weaponize it and blackmail political enemies. "Massive surveillance thwarts citizens pressuring for political change through the risk of criminal prosecution, blackmail, or other threats," Granick explains (Granick 2017, p.8).

The only reason Americans know about the extent to which the United States government has illegally spied is because of Snowden, a prodigy hacker-turned-NSA-agent-turned-whistleblower, who chose to sacrifice a cushy life in America with a girlfriend, top-level clearance, and a six-figure paycheck.

"I believe that at this point in history, the greatest danger to our freedom and way of life comes from the reasonable fear of omniscient State powers kept in check by nothing more than policy documents," Snowden said. "These protocols are complicated and secret. When people break them, it has taken the public years to find out, and no one gets punished."

Barton Gellman and Sam Adler-Bell explain in an article for The Century Foundation:

"Federal, state, and local governments shield their high-technology operations with stealth, obfuscation, and sometimes outright lies when obliged to answer questions. In many cases, perhaps most, these defenses defeat attempts to extract a full, concrete accounting of what the government knows about us, and how it puts that information to use. There is a lot less mystery for the poor and disfavored, for whom surveillance takes palpable, often frightening forms."

We need to reinstate privacy protections. Privacy belongs to individuals, while the powerful government must be transparent. Moreover, in the 1980s "The Right to Privacy," published in the *Harvard Law Review* Brandeis and Samuel D. Warren argued for a "right to be let alone" derived from English Common Law.

In 1928, associate justice of the US Supreme Court, Brandeis, dissented in *Olmstead v. United States*, which upheld a warrantless wiretap because police had not trespassed on the defendant's property or searched his "tangible material effects."

Brandeis wrote the Founders were less concerned with "material things" than government overreach into our private lives.

"They sought to protect Americans in their beliefs, their thoughts, their emotions, and their sensations," he wrote.

"They conferred, as against the government, the right to be let alone—the most comprehensive of rights and the right most valued by civilized men."

He said an "unjustifiable intrusion," whether or not by physical trespass, breached the Fourth Amendment, and created illegally, "must be deemed a violation of the Fifth" (ibid.).

CHAPTER 4

HOW BIG TECH GOT CREEPY

———

When I first accessed AOL.com dial-up internet, I was dumbfounded. After ten or twenty minutes, at least half of a page of a novel internet was just a few clicks away. Despite slow service, you could download any music (and viruses) from Limewire, search for directions across the country on MapQuest, or anything you could imagine. The internet utterly awestruck me, and it hopefully always will. I could live chat with friends and crushes, take over the world playing *Age of Empires*, and get a thrill playing *DOOM*, and it seemed like magic. Moreover, I could chat with any stranger, search for the answer to any question, and peek at how large and complex the world is.

Even if my local library didn't have books on niche topics like internet policy or implications of US Supreme Court cases, I could sometimes find them online. My personal favorite throwback to the early internet was logging onto AOL.com to hear a booming voice say, "You've got mail!" back when email was exciting instead of a seemingly black hole filled mostly with spam. My current Gmail inbox has more than 37,000 unread messages.

At that time, phone plans came with limited text messages. A camera, calculator, and recorder were separate from a phone. So, the evolution of unlimited minutes and texts was incredible; not to mention most phones can tether the internet at a moment's notice—possibly the most helpful tool for journalists filing stories in unusual spots like Lollapalooza.

Despite being ten-plus years ago, I remember every one of my closest friends' online usernames: Joey Weber's (Run-2fast4you_95@hotmail.com), Tony Talley's (tony.talley@hotmail.com), Jeff Talley (Jeff_2200@hotmail.com), and Denton Williams (cubsfan33@gmail.com).

Initially, the internet and tech companies seemed like they could only do good, like their spread was synonymous with freedom and democracy. The companies championed freedom of speech, free information, and access to anyone with an internet connection. Thanks to Uber and Lyft, you can get a ride in most urban places, even if it's expensive. Google Docs meant you don't have to pay substantial costs for Microsoft Word to send a document via email.

But fast forward ten years later, and tech companies twisted into a scrawling monster that tracks everything ranging from tracking menstrual cycles to what podcasts we listen to and what we watch on YouTube. Between 2011 and 2021, tech evolved into the creepiest entity on Earth—and an absolute nightmare when abused by bad actors.

In 2015, Indiana resident James Maier started working as a janitor to pay his bills and cash-flow college to leap into a political consultant role after. He spent twelve years building a 5,000-person Facebook network of like-minded conservatives and libertarians. Then Facebook permanently banned his account after three strikes. The first ban, Maier thinks, was for mentioning he had a specific gun part. Not even that he was going to sell it illegally, or that he was going to shoot up a place—just for alleged possession (despite what coastal residents think, gun ownership is frequent in flyover country).

The second strike was for Maier calling someone "dumb," he alleges, what Facebook apparently considers "hate speech." The third was unclear. Facebook didn't respond to multiple requests for comment. However, Maier said he shared several Babylon Bee articles a few days before the permanent ban, which Facebook notified him were "fake news."

Social media companies became creepy once they started banning people for minor disagreements and insults, and choosing who wins disputes. Both Facebook's algorithms and human censors seem to lack a sense of humor. In July 2021, Facebook slapped a one-day ban on a Metro Detroit woman for commenting on a meme that women notice nail polish shades better than men, writing, "Why are men so stupid?" Facebook deemed the harmless sentence "hate speech" (Dupnack 2021). Facebook and most social media companies need to learn how to take a joke—Section 230 protects them from many lawsuits anyway.

They also spy on us as much as possible. While I was celebrating my friend landing a big-time lawyer gig in Washington,

DC, my friends suggested I drink a can of hard kombucha. For the next five days, my phone bombarded me with ads ranging from Facebook to Gmail. What else is Big Tech listening to, and who are they selling information to?

I care about the power of big tech companies because often, we use Google searches as a form of a history lesson—searching when certain people died, the height of rapper Snoop Dogg, or what year a war ended. But some search engines abuse this function at the request of embarrassed governments. Microsoft-owned search engine Bing hid any image results to US users who searched for the term "tank man" on June 4, 2021, the thirty-two-year anniversary of the 1989 Tiananmen Square massacre in which the Chinese government murdered anywhere between a few hundred to a few thousand protesting citizens (Campbell 2021). It's best known for an iconic image of a single man, alone, holding a suitcase standing in front of dozens of tanks. However, Microsoft told *The Verge*, "This is due to an accidental human error, and we are actively working to resolve this" (ibid.).

That's a common refrain for tech companies that want no paper trail and won't admit guilt. Oftentimes, these tech companies won't even notify you of a changed action like reinstating your account, just to cover its ass.

SOCIAL INFLUENCERS?
In just a span of ten years, major online companies realized how much influence they held over consumers. Tech companies once competed for customers. But now that they have so many, the companies focus on censoring and influencing us (or at least try to).

When Marine and American hero Kareem Nikoui, twenty years old, died in action in Kabul, Afghanistan, on August 26, 2020, his mother was distraught. Shana Chappell took to social media in a viral post to air her grievances over one person responsible for his death: President Joe Biden. The same day, Facebook and Twitter suspended her accounts. A Facebook spokesperson tells me it was a mistake. "We express our deepest condolences to Ms. Chappell and her family," the person wrote in an email. "Her tribute to her heroic son does not violate any of our policies. While the post was not removed, her account was incorrectly deleted and we have since restored it."

After working in journalism for more than ten years, I've calibrated a pretty good bullshit detector. When I'm talking with these Facebook, Instagram, and TikTok spokespeople, that meter is usually reading at an all-time high. Many Big Tech spokespeople won't even let you use their name, which is another red flag. One quote from internal Facebook documents published by *The Wall Street Journal* confirmed my suspicion.

A 2019 internal review of Facebook's whitelisting practices of whom they let break its rules marked "attorney-client privileged" described Facebook's as widespread and "not publicly defensible" (Horowitz 2021).

"We are not actually doing what we say we do publicly," said the confidential review. It called the company's actions "a breach of trust" and added, "Unlike the rest of our community, these people can violate our standards without any consequences" (ibid.).

After pressure from *The Wall Street Journal*, Facebook and Instagram have been placed in the spotlight in 2021, and for good reason. Facebook can be used for evil. The majority of online recruitment in active sex trafficking cases in the US last year took place on Facebook, according to the Human Trafficking Institute's 2020 Federal Human Trafficking Report.

"The internet has become the dominant tool that traffickers use to recruit victims, and they often recruit them on a number of very common social networking websites," Human Trafficking Institute CEO Victor Boutros said on CBSN. "Facebook overwhelmingly is used by traffickers to recruit victims in active sex trafficking cases" (Elkind 2021).

TECH COMPANIES INVADING AND STEALING YOUR DATA

Companies buy up your data for unknown reasons. TikTok will pay a ninety-two-million-dollar settlement for harvesting personal data including facial recognition without consent from users as young as six years old sharing the data with third parties, some based in China (Allyn 2021). The proposed settlement applies to eighty-nine million TikTok users in the US whose personal data was allegedly tracked and sold illegally to advertisers according to a plaintiff's settlement obtained by NPR. The violation is a reoccurring theme: In February 2019, TikTok paid a $5.7 million fine to the Federal Trade Commission for allegedly collecting children's personal information (FTC 2019).

Google and YouTube in 2019 also paid a record $170 million to settle allegations by the Federal Trade Commission and the New York Attorney General that YouTube illegally collected children's personal information without parental consent (FTC 2019). For example, Google and YouTube told Mattel, maker of Barbie and Monster High toys, "YouTube is today's leader in reaching children ages six to eleven against top TV channels" and told Hasbro, which makes My Little Pony and Play-Doh, that YouTube is the "#1 website regularly visited by kids" (ibid.).

HOME SWEET HOME?

In law, a man's home is like his castle. We wouldn't let a stranger listen in to our most intimate moments, but we keep Alexas in multiple rooms of our house. The personal technology we use knows our deepest secrets. A Harvard Berkman Klein Center for Internet & Society research report found smart appliances with sensors and more could open the door to "numerous avenues for government actors to demand access to real-time and recorded communications (Zuboff 2019).

Loosely explained, the Internet of Things is the concept of connecting devices with sensors to the internet like home security systems, smart TVs, Alexas, fridges, the thermostat, and more that exchange data. So, we have more data than ever, but we're basically placing surveillance inside our homes as well. Just how Alexa hears us when we ask her what the weather forecast is, she can also hear us talk about other private matters.

In 2020, experts estimate the installation of thirty-one billion Internet of Things devices. By 2021, thirty-five billion

IoT devices will be installed worldwide. By 2025, more than seventy-five billion IoT devices will be connected to the web (Maayan 2020). The more devices we have, the more vulnerable we are to unwanted surveillance.

In 2009, 15-year-old high schooler Blake Robbins was accused of dealing or consuming drugs. But that behavior originated inside his own home, and was captured through the camera of his school-issued computer Pennsylvania's Lower Merion School District, according to a lawsuit filed by Robbins. Since the COVID-19 pandemic, schools give students laptop computers contingent on a privacy policy that allows school districts to spy on the children at home, even going as far as to activate webcams.

Robbins was actually just eating candy.

For fun in 2013, reporter Kashmir Hill hacked into smart homes and turned off lights in a home 600 miles away, and if connected to the Internet of Things, could have controlled hot tubs, garage doors, and video surveillance (Mitnick 2017, p.201).

Tech-driven houses and smart cities constantly collect data for almost every appliance, from beds to washing machines. If we're not careful, smart houses will collect every piece of data it can on humans. Collecting light data can show someone has trouble sleeping. Loud music plus the genre could market to party gifts. Frequent sex could buy ad time for birth control, sex toys, or children's toys.

It's ironic each person's DVD or video game rental history is private, but not our most personal data such as our credit card purchases.

In 1988, Congress passed the Video Privacy Protection Act (VPPA) to prevent "wrongful disclosure of video tape rental or sale records" after Robert Bork's video rental history was published during his Supreme Court nomination. It makes any "video tape service provider" that discloses rental information outside the ordinary course of business liable for up to $2,500 in actual damages (ibid.).

So existing law protects our video rentals, but not our credit card purchases.

Tech activist Liz O'Sullivan is Amazon's new product called Sidewalk, which is a wireless mesh Wi-Fi network that will help link connected devices at a long-range. On September 26, 2019, O'Sullivan tweeted that products like Sidewalk (which is in a testing phase) need only a small fraction of the country to opt into a network covering our neighborhoods and streets." Her takeaway: "Amazon is building the infrastructure to monitor us all."

A majority of these appliances will be in our homes, and we can use the technology to lock our doors, dim lights, turn on the television, and spy on the kids.

Every decision in life is a tradeoff. Installing a Ring doorbell can provide peace of mind, evidence of crimes, and help track perpetrators. It could also be used to spy on you and equip thieves with information to heist your valuables. Downloading video to the cloud effectively centralizes the information for an attacker—or the government—to access. We literally pay tech companies, and by proxy, give the government access and the means to spy on us. "Smart" homes are basically data harvesting to the extreme, with no terms and conditions or limits.

The more we advance, the more tech can limit us rather than enable us. We seem to limit our lives around our phone and laptop battery or phone and internet connection, but that shouldn't stop us from charging ahead. It's healthy to unplug from phone and internet access.

The more connections we have, the more vulnerabilities there are. Google Nests have smart thermostats that adapt to user behavior patterns and to what's going on in the power grid. It tracks humidity, ambient light, and movement. Some fridges can even track food expiration, but your Foscam baby monitors can also be hacked. Soon, your trash can could snitch on you for not recycling. A majority of these appliances will be in our homes, and we can use technology to lock our doors, dim lights, turn on the television, and spy on the kids. Former US Director of National Intelligence James Clapper told Congress in 2016 that intelligence services might use the "Internet of Things" for "identification, surveillance, monitoring, location tracking, and targeting for recruitment, or to gain access to networks or user credentials" (Ackerman and Thielman 2016). The same walls that marked our territory, where law enforcement and tech companies couldn't penetrate, now box us in. Under current data laws, if we surround ourselves with smart tech, we're just giving the government our data. When the Bill of Rights was written, we could be safe from outside intrusion inside our home. But slowly, that place of solitude is changing to where our belongings are digital and can be accessed from anywhere. We can be watched at all times, depending on the tech we keep around us.

Now, we keep microphones that spy on us in our bedrooms through cellphones, Alexas, and even fridges equipped with microphones. Connect a phone to a car, and it knows who we call, who we text, and what kind of music and podcasts we listen to. If you only use minimal technology, this might not be a problem. One-off data isn't very helpful unless you have additional context. But the more data points you can gather—Google searches, heart rate Fitbit data, what movies and TV shows you've watched, your driving record for a certain day—much can be deduced. Data brokers buy this information and package it—including your name, home address, age, religion, education level, and income to sell to interested parties (Macmillan 2019).

Google and Facebook know a lot about you—what you Googled late at night, which profiles you stalk, and your deepest medical worries, but they lack the force of government to imprison, fine, or kill you.

Nostalgia of the old (and crappy) internet is good, but we have to bring a more cynical analysis of the current internet today. Is this Nigerian Prince emailing me really going to give me three million dollars? We must be more careful about the information we give out and adjust our privacy settings. In the last three months, I've seen my friends get scammed out of hundreds of dollars through a fake but similar Venmo account, ripped off through a false vendor selling concert tickets, and a family member fall for a phishing scam for someone claiming to be the US Census Bureau. Trust, but verify.

Edward Snowden explained in an interview with John Stossel about the implication of your workplace and the general public knowing your personal information.

"What happens when your workplace knows? What happens when your government knows? Who decides what is normal, what's acceptable, and what's not? We can do things that are very common today, or we can have positions or interests that are very uncommon today, but harmless," Snowden said. (Stossel 2020, 36:40).

Snowden makes a great point. We should consider the worst possible outcomes with information we willingly place on the internet, like our mother's maiden name or other frequent identity verification methods that could be used to hack your personal accounts.

"In a free society, we are allowed to be different," Snowden said. "We are allowed to be weird. We can be strange, as long as we're not hurting anyone else." (ibid. 27:04).

CHAPTER 5

BIG TECH "TYRANNY"

———

"All animals are equal but some are more equal than others."
—(ORWELL 1945).

Take two people: one rich and connected, the other poor, and your average person. Both can post the same false content on social media, but for the most part, only the poor and less influential is banned and censored. That's the takeaway from *The Wall Street Journal*'s expose of internal Facebook documents about its "XCheck program that shields high-profile accounts including celebrities, politicians, and journalists from the company's normal enforcement process (Horowitz 2021).

"We are not actually doing what we say we do publicly," said the confidential review. It called the company's actions "a breach of trust" and added, "Unlike the rest of our community, these people can violate our standards without any consequences" (ibid.).

These are the stories of the people on the other side that Facebook gags and shuts down their account, often vanquishing priceless family photos, final conversations with loved ones, and business contacts after being kicked off social media because Facebook couldn't take a joke or a meme. Even worse, these users don't have the power to fight back. Once Facebook denies an appeal, there's not much you can do. I find it ironic that a company that claims to be woke but discriminates against its average users by giving an edge to the wealthy and celebrities as opposed to smaller users who don't bring in comparative revenue and that don't have a big enough platform to reach front-page news.

Many people have lost priceless family items—jewelry, photos of loved ones, or more in fires and natural disasters. But now, people are losing photos, businesses, and final conversations with loved ones after being kicked off social media.

"I have lost so many memories of my children and my father who has passed away that are irreplaceable," Tori Loafman, a Michigan mother, told me.

She's not alone.

Mary Magadelene, a small business owner and entrepreneur, used Facebook to promote her hustles to a few thousand friends and family until Facebook deleted her account in January, citing community standards violations. She lost all her photos, messages, and business contacts. She was never told which standard she violated or which post.

Kyle Moody, a ten-year veteran, says his Facebook, Instagram, YouTube, Twitter, and Google accounts were all deleted on the same day on or about October 2020. "It was so abrupt," he said. "They didn't give me any warning." Afterward, his conversations weren't viewable by either party. He doesn't want to use Facebook, he just wants information and pictures of his late stepfather, who was a Vietnam vet. He had roughly 10,000 pictures across all his digital platforms, and he bought a photo printer for copies, but not before Facebook deleted him. "It wasn't in response to one issue," he told me.

A lot of activists were kicked off on the same day, many who knew each other and interacted with each other's posts. He thinks it was a targeted attack.

Moody just wants his account reinstated for forty-eight hours so he can get his messages, pictures, and business contact information and then leave. But Facebook hasn't answered his or my questions—a common theme when it comes to Big Tech companies. Moody believes he was part of a larger group of "voluntaryists" who were kicked off in 2020 for posting anti-statist memes. Or it could have been related to a *Trailer Park Boys* group he co-founded six years ago that grew to 130,000 people.

The group has been penalized for posting screenshots of the show. One of Moody's last posts was a screenshot from the show that "Corey and Jacob got fooled by trannies," and received a ninety-day ban for "hate speech." The last three bans Moody received weren't for political speech but were for *Trailer Park Boys* memes quoting the show that Facebook deemed as 'hate speech.'"

"It's a joke. It's from the show," Moody said. "I'm in a private group, joking with people who love the show, about the show.

Nobody forced them to be in the group." Moody does moderate hateful speech on the page, which he argues is much different from jokes. "There's good-hearted joking, and then there's hatefulness," he told me. Therefore, Facebook will allow a group based on a TV show that promotes "hate speech" but you can't post screenshots or jokes from the show within the group. Does that make sense?

To be clear, private companies can do what they want. Therefore, Facebook can censor whomever it pleases, and restaurants can either kick you out for not wearing a mask or for wearing a mask. And that's a good thing if you've seen a drunk person harassing women at a bar, screaming pejoratives, and trying to start fights. Can you imagine if a company was forced to serve a client? Companies, like people, are complex and we're not entitled to its services. However, tech companies should enact clear standards for blocking and banning people. And if companies like Facebook, Instagram, and Twitter continue to needlessly censor people for petty comments, we should leave the platform.

Ex-Google employee and Big Tech critic Tristan Harris told the Senate Judiciary Committee that the business model of big social media companies "is to create a society that is addicted, outraged, [and] polarized" (Conklin 2021).

Breaking news as a reporter is hard enough, but if Big Tech doesn't like you, it's nearly impossible. In December 2020, Twitter blocked the sharing of dozens of legitimate news outlets (Krug 2020). The Center Square Illinois reporter Greg Bishop, who has covered state government for more than a decade, broke the news about newly released documents from the ComEd bribery scandal for which it pleaded guilty to federal charges and agreed to pay a $200 million fine (ibid.).

But Twitter blocked the link, plugging one of the quickest ways to share the news, and wouldn't say why. Much like the Wizard of Oz, the Twitter overlords operate from behind a curtain of vague algorithms, arbitrary blocking rules, and most importantly, providing little to no transparency. Twitter wouldn't allow me (or my colleagues) to share The Center Square articles on Twitter. They didn't even tell us, and we violated no known policy (ibid.). I rarely post on social media, but I use them daily to stay in touch with a wide-ranging network of professional and personal friends.

I have about 12,000 connections on LinkedIn, only a few hundred Twitter followers, and 1,867 friends on Facebook. Facebook sourced nearly half ($2,500) of my book preorders, and likely will source an even larger portion for future books. In the digital age, social media plays a crucial role in journalism. Journalists break news via Twitter to other journalists with an unhealthy Twitter addiction and push alerts enabled, and it just takes one retweet of a profile with a high follower count to start a viral post.

If one of the tech giants kicks you off, one of your greatest personal distributions to your network is annihilated. Your Facebook friends are much more likely to read the articles you share compared to a stranger, and Facebook groups provide an immense source for research. With one click, you can share your article with thousands of people compared to sending it to each person by email. Social media allows for a snowball effect for sharing news and other items.

If you're banned from Facebook and Twitter, your reach is greatly diminished, and you lose daily touch with your network that spans high school friends to college professors to someone you met on a plane. Writers' jobs are to get read, not to write. Companies like Facebook and Instagram can demonetize people's accounts, place warning markers, and more. But finally, people are starting to fight back. Veteran reporter John Stossel, who's won nineteen Emmys, sued Facebook and a few fact-checkers in September 2021 over defamation (Spangler 2021). For more than a year, Facebook has shadowbanned his videos, placed warning labels on them, and dropped monthly Facebook revenue from $10,000 to $5,500 (ibid.).

Stossel explained why he was suing in a Facebook post.

"I get that Facebook faces lots of lawsuits, including ridiculous claims from people with bad agendas. It's hard for Facebook to clean up its site. But I know fact-checking. I've spent fifty years as a journalist sorting through the hype and fear to share what is true. It's labor intensive to unemotionally look through data to investigate a scare-story, a process that my team and the people I trust have gotten quite good at. By contrast, when Facebook empowers activist 'Fact Checkers' who double down when they are wrong; that's just wrong" (Stossel 2021).

He explained further. "I hate lawsuits. But last week, I sued Facebook and their 'fact-checker' Climate Feedback. I sued because they LIED in multiple careless 'fact-checks,' throttled my channel, and because they frequently smear others too. It needs to stop" (Stossel 2021).

Big Tech companies like TikTok are even silencing the opinion of medical doctors. Medical Doctor Scott Jensen, sixty-six years old, downloaded TikTok to reach young voters in his 2022 gubernatorial challenge of Minnesota Governor Tim Walz. In three weeks, Jensen garnered more than 286,000 followers and 1.2 million likes on TikTok. Over 100,000 people were viewing his videos daily. But he was "permanently banned" for violating community standards that "prohibit medical misinformation, and this account was removed due to repeated violations of this policy," TikTok's Jamie Favazza emailed me. His account had four or so videos inactivated, but some were reversed upon appeal. "We never had any warnings or anything," Jensen told me.

TikTok's Community Guidelines "apply to everyone and to everything on TikTok," Favazza said, even a thirty-two-year veteran family doctor who won the 2016 Family Physician of the Year from the Minnesota Academy of Family Physicians (Olson 2016).

However, internal TikTok documents show it tells moderators to censor content from people they believed to be ugly, overweight, disabled, or poor, the Intercept reported on March 16, 2020. Clearly, they don't treat everyone fairly or enforce Community Standards equally.

The day Jensen's account was banned, it posted a video criticizing "60 Minutes" for a hit job on Florida Governor Ron DeSantis, where they deceptively edited an interview alleging he helped Publix get more doses of the COVID-19 vaccine because of campaign donations. But after it was exposed, "60 Minutes" deleted the story (Moore 2021). It's a mystery which posts violated which rule, part of Big Tech's veil of secrecy to avoid further criticism. Jensen guessed one strike was when he said taking the COVID-19 vaccine should be a personal choice—that's his opinion. He disagrees he was spreading COVID-19 misinformation. "If I said the Moderna vaccine wasn't effective in any way, that could be misinformation because efficacy must be defined as to what the vaccine is supposed to do, e.g., stop transmission or stop death."

TikTok partners with fact-checking organizations that help assess the accuracy of content accredited by the International Fact-Checking Network, which ranges across ninety-two organizations, over six countries, and includes SciVerify, Lead Stories, and Politifact (Poynter 2021).

TFCN is a project of the Florida-based Poynter Institue, a left-leaning organization that strives to improve journalism (ibid.). (Disclosure: I was a fellow in one of Poynter's journalism programs, but not that project). I can attest to the quality of Poynter's instruction and network of legendary writers including Roy Peter Clark who improve younger writers.

Attempting to moderate social media is hard. More than 400 hours of content are uploaded to YouTube each minute (Jarboe 2015). Facebook has about 350 million photos a day added to its platform (Smith 2013). It would be nearly impossible to view each piece of content before it was uploaded to the site. Many uploads are memes, including a lawyer joke that Facebook banned Nicholas Somberg, the "Bearded Libertarian Lawyer" of Michigan, for seven days. I wasn't able to include the following memes in this book because of copyright law. The first meme showed one person who stormed the US Capitol on January 6, 2021, and stole a lectern. Facebook claimed the joke equated to "supporting terrorism."

Facebook "permanently" deleted Somberg's account in March 2021 for posting a photoshopped meme of Michigan Governor Gretchen Whitmer fully clothed onto the Pornhub site with the title, "GROSS SLUT FUCKS WHOLE STATE," referring to the economic devastation from COVID-19 and the longest and strictest-in-the-Midwest rules enacted by the first-term Democratic governor to combat the virus (McClallen 2021).

Facebook gave Somberg no recourse, saying the post was "sexual exploitation." Twelve years of content, direct messages, and advertising were "forever down the memory hole," Somberg said. Until they magically reversed the decision on April 17, 2021, five days after I started asking questions, but the platform never admitted they reinstated his account because they didn't want the email admitting guilt.

Ironically, a similar post went viral on April 20, 2021, after a jury convicted former Minneapolis police officer Derek Chauvin on charges of second-degree unintentional murder, third-degree murder, and second-degree manslaughter in the death of George Floyd. The photoshopped meme showed Chauvin fully clothed being handcuffed with the Pornhub header "Dirty cop gets fucked by Jury," and was shared 26,000 times.

Are there different standards of "sexual exploitation" for men versus women? Somberg thinks so. "Proof positive it's not about what you say, but WHO you say it about. The censorship is real."

He believes private companies can set their own rules, but Facebook also gets widespread government immunity through Section 230 for moderating content as they please. That feature aimed to jumpstart online activity and prevent social media companies from being sued into bankruptcy. Somberg argues Facebook is nearly a public square now, comparing its service to a public utility like water or electricity, which can't deny access to customers based on the customer's beliefs.

"They're almost a public square now. The line is blurred, in my opinion," Somberg said. "Can Verizon deny you service because they don't like what you're talking about on the phone?" There's a difference between being refused cell phone service and a utility like water or energy, but as we'll see, being kicked off Facebook can have severe implications such as losing customers and general public exposure. Getting kicked off Facebook can kill a business, especially one that relies on ad revenue, just because Facebook can't take a joke.

The First Amendment protects satire, a market as old as time now comprised of *The Onion*, the Babylon Bee, and the Velvet Hamster and all internet memes—businesses that use parody to prove points. Still, places like *The New York Times* have accused the hilarious sites of spreading misinformation (I'm not sure how a newspaper can have such a fundamental misunderstanding of the First Amendment) (Mike 2021). Social media sites across the board have threatened to kick off parody Christian news site the Babylon Bee multiple times for doing its job: making hilarious jokes.

Facebook threatened to kick The Bee off the platform and demonetize them after Snopes, a twenty-five-year-old fact-checking company, felt the need to debunk an article titled "CNN Purchases Industrial-Sized Washing Machine to Spin News Before Publication," which claimed the device allowed "CNN reporters to load just the facts of a given issue, turn a dial to "spin cycle," and within five minutes, receive a nearly unrecognizable version of the story that's been spun to fit with the news station's agenda" (Mikkelson 2018). Facebook later apologized.

"For one thing, it's the most ridiculous story to fact check. It's not even remotely believable," Babylon Bee CEO Seth Dillon told me about Snopes fact-checking The Bee's article "CNN Purchases Industrial-Sized Washing Machine to Spin News Before Publication."

Facebook contracted with Snopes as an "independent fact-checker" and twenty-seven other companies through the Facebook Journalism Program. In September 2020, *USA Today* felt the need to fact check a Bee piece, titled "Ninth Circuit Court Overturns Death of Ruth Bader Ginsberg" (Cox 2020).

In March 2021, *New York Times* technology columnist Mike Isaac slammed The Bee as a "far-right misinformation site" that "sometimes trafficked in misinformation under the guise of satire." Dillon disagrees.

"For better or worse, *The New York Times* is considered a reliable source, so it matters what they say about us," Dillon said. "If their false statements about us are allowed to stand, then the next thing you know, our Wikipedia page will say we traffic in misinformation, and it will cite *The New York Times* for support. This is how they establish difficult-to-rebutt false narratives about sites they don't like," Dillon said about the *NYT* saying The Bee was a "far-right misinformation site that "sometimes trafficked in misinformation under the guise of satire." "The great irony is that they're using misinformation to smear us as being a source of it."

The Bee's primary means of generating traffic, like most media organizations, is through social media. Dillon said he'd been concerned the site will be kicked off the platform. While Facebook can kick off actual fake news, Dillon argued there should be a separate category for satire. On May 5, 2021, Facebook restricted The Bee's monetization and reach for sharing an article about how Dr. Anthony Fauci said we could stop wearing masks as soon as humans evolved their own masks, flagging the story as "harmful misinformation."

"It's a joke," Dillon told me. "I can't get over how ridiculous it is. It used to be that jokes were either funny or not. Now, we're giving them a truth rating."

It's not a game to The Bee, which has to make $100,000 monthly payroll so employees can pay rent and feed families. Twitter has suspended them before, but they said it was a mistake and reversed their decision but explained none of it to the suspended company. However, the damage is already done to The Bee's reputation, and if they're kicked off for good, it'll diminish The Bee's reach.

However, *The New York Times* apparently remembered they are a newspaper, which is supposed to champion free speech, and in early June issued an apology and corrected the article. Many people don't understand satire—they think it's fake news, misleading to people, or defamation, but it's none of those and plays a unique role.

"Satire is able to get at the truth from a different angle," Dillon told me. "G.K. Chesterton once said, 'Humor can get under the door while seriousness is still fumbling at the handle.' I think he's right. Humor is disarming, and that's what makes it so effective. It can slip past your defenses in a way that rational arguments never could."

While arguments often escalate to shouting matches and breaking things, satire hits calmly and quietly.

"I think humor is disarming in a way that more serious arguments and posts aren't," Dillon said. "Even, especially in really controversial topics if you're dealing with something like race or abortion or same-sex marriage or whatever the hot topic is."

Dillon said he thinks the nexus of their worldview—a Christian conservative perspective—is a driving force behind the bans and threats since enforcement often depends on the topic.

"Depending on the target of the joke, there's a much greater chance that it's going to be fact checked. If Biden or other prominent Democrats are the target, it's highly likely that it's going to get fact checked. If we're making fun of Trump, they don't seem care. They don't mind if people believe those jokes are true. And, of course, anything related to the pandemic is heavily scrutinized," Dillon said.

It's hard to tell if Big Tech actually does censor specific political viewpoints, but a recent Pew Research Center survey found that nearly three-quarters of US adults believe social media sites intentionally censor political viewpoints. In the last two years, at least two congressional hearings have focused on the question of tech censorship.

On the other hand, Facebook's top ten sites are frequently conservative, and a 2019 review of over 400 political pages on Facebook by the left-leaning media watchdog Media Matters found conservative pages performed about equally as well as liberal ones (Whitehouse 2019).

However, reliable data is scarce, and social media platforms are tight-lipped about decision-making content moderation to avoid criticism and provide as little ammunition as possible to critics. Nevertheless, you don't need mass amounts of data to see what's going on is wrong and blatant abuse of power, even if the companies are acting within their power. We may feel powerless against these faceless companies, but we can always unplug from them and communicate with friends and family via different platforms, through the app Signal or text messages. Facebook is powerful because of the network effect, meaning the more friends you have on it, the more useful it is to you, but that works the opposite as well. The more we detach, the more power consumers take from Big Tech Tyranny.

CHAPTER 6

BIG TECH'S BETRAYAL

—————

When the *New York Post* broke a story implicating Hunter Biden pre-2020 presidential election, Twitter banned the *NYP*—America's oldest continuously published newspaper founded by Alexander Hamilton—for sixteen days (Golding 2020). Take into account Twitter's apparent motto as of June 29, 2021: "Twitter is an open service that's home to a world of diverse people, perspectives, ideas, and information" (Twitter 2020).

That is unless you say something that doesn't line up with Big Tech. Twitter CEO Jack Dorsey later admitted Twitter botched the decision, but that was too little too late. Dorsey founded Twitter as a free speech platform but uses it to suppress free speech.

"Our communication around our actions on the @nypost article was not great," Dorsey tweeted on October 14, 2020. "And blocking URL sharing via tweet or DM with zero context as to why we're blocking: unacceptable."

YouTube's mission is "to give everyone a voice and show them the world. We believe that everyone deserves to have a voice, and that the world is a better place when we listen, share, and build community through our stories. Our values are based on four essential freedoms that define who we are."

YouTube's actions are starkly different. YouTube removed a video of Florida Governor Ron Desantis and Ivy League experts' opinions on COVID-19 because it contradicted federal health guidelines (Wilson and Ross 2021).

The March 18, 2021 roundtable featured physicians critical of the government's response to the COVID-19 pandemic—Dr. Scott Atlas, a radiologist and pandemic adviser to former President Donald Trump; Dr. Martin Kulldorff of Harvard University; Dr. Sunetra Gupta of Oxford University; and Dr. Jay Bhattacharya of Stanford Medical School.

So, who's right? Pulling that video removed the voices of extremely well-educated experts from the community, directly violating YouTube's mission. Is the general public so naive that we should censor people saying stupid things online? If so, we should cancel most television.

A new motto for Twitter could be: "It's what's happening (if we like it)."

Don't get me wrong: Twitter is an incredible tool for disseminating information quickly best shown through journalism Twitter—which is why Twitter is banned completely in Nigeria, China, and Iran, and is intermittently blocked in dozens more (Walsh 2021). But Twitter's network effect augments if people with a range of beliefs can use it, although private companies can do what they want.

Founded in 2004, Facebook's mission is "to give people the power to build community and bring the world closer together. People use Facebook to stay connected with friends and family, to discover what's going on in the world, and to share and express what matters to them."

Unless what matters to them is conservative politics. In 2016, Facebook placed on leave and then fired wunderkind Palmer Luckey, who founded Oculus VR as a teenager and sold it to the Tech giant, all because he donated $10,000 to support then-presidential candidate Donald Trump. Facebook denies this, but a one-hundred-million-dollar lawsuit settlement with Luckey says otherwise (Bokhari 2020).

Similarly, Facebook hit Michigan attorney Nick Somberg with a thirty-day penalty just for comparing two screenshots of news stories. On one side was the arrest of FBI Special Agent Richard Trask, arrested for alleged domestic violence who smashed his wife's head into a nightstand "several times" and choking her afterward (Brand-Williams 2020). Trask was released on a $10,000 personal recognizance bond and faces a charge punishable by up to ten years in prison (ibid.). On the other was a screenshot of Joseph Morrison's bond, a man the government alleged made a terrorist threat and provided material support for terrorist acts, meaning letting people train with firearms on his property. He initially got a ten-million-dollar bond later dropped to $150,000—still fifteen times that of the man who allegedly beat, choked, and bloodied his wife's head (McClallen 2021). "If only he beat his wife instead of posting memes," Somberg commented before he was banned for "violence against women."

Not all posts are scrutinized so heavily. Meanwhile on September 16, 2021, *The Wall Street Journal* reported a cartel's Instagram posting executions, people beaten and tied to a chair, and a bag full of severed hands were left up for five months.

GOOGLE

The motto "Don't be evil" seems pretty self-explanatory, but it means different things to different people. When Donald Trump won the 2016 presidential election, the classic Big Tech companies were shaken, holding multiple sessions to talk about their feelings and swearing to fight what they saw as the new president's "evil" values (Bokhari 2020, p.14).

Then-president of Alphabet, Google's parent company, Sergey Brin, suggested using Jigsaw, a search engine manipulation tool, to solve what he calls "extremism," or what most people call the average interests in the Midwest, including shooting guns in cornfields for fun, loving God, and distrusting the government (ibid.., p. 16).

In 2018, a Google whistleblower leaked a document from Google's internal Insight Labs titled "The Good Censor" (ibid.., 27).

"Free speech has become a social, economic, and political weapon," the authors of one of the most powerful companies on Earth wrote. They argued the free internet gave a level playing field to "have-a-go commentators" and "authoritative voices"—what they called a threat to "rational debate" (ibid.., 27).

But who decides what voices are authoritative?

GET OUT OF JAIL FREE CARDS

Tech companies seem to have a get-out-of-jail card with Congress and the courts, whether because of arguments or political donations. As Peter Harter, cofounder of the company Markup, which provides public policy solutions to lawmakers and regulators, said, "These companies get so powerful and have so much money and access to politicians and employee talent that the usual rules don't apply" (Foroohar 2019, p. 105).

These tech behemoths should instead let consumers think for themselves and remember why they were founded. Companies like Facebook and Twitter are growing so large they're turning into government-esque entities that wrongly attempt to control every part of society. The days of Google's "Don't be evil" motto are dead as companies focus more on market share than innovation and pull the rug from underneath small companies. Most Silicon Valley tech giants have relocated physically and morally from the days of a scrappy startup. Now, they suppress smaller companies, steal from competitors, and invade other sectors to use scale, vertical integration, and complexity to crush other companies.

In 2017, the European Union fined Google 2.4 billion euro for anticompetitive conduct, finding "Google has systematically given prominent placement to its own comparison-shopping service" while it "demoted rival comparison shopping services in its search results" (Hawley 2021, p. 118). Google initially partnered to help sites like Yelp but eventually stabbed them in the back according to a 2012 Federal Trade Commission report saying Google stole from Yelp, TripAdvisor, and Amazon (ibid.., p. 133). While the stated purpose of social media is to unite us, it more often seems to divide us if it   ismore profitable. Former YouTube engineer Guillaume Chaslot developed an algorithm to pop the site's "filter bubble," which YouTube dropped because it would have resulted in lower "watch time" (Foroohar 2019, 53).

Tech companies take more of our time by prioritizing emotionally charged, sometimes out-of-context content, especially videos that autoplay as you scroll. Moreover, companies like Facebook experiment on users constantly, attempting to affect emotions via algorithms. These companies don't care about your mental health. They just want your attention, your data, and for no one to notice they're essentially stealing people's data.

In 2018, Apple CEO Tim Cook told EU officials: "We shouldn't sugar-coat the consequences. This is surveillance. And these stockpiles of personal data only serve to enrich the companies that collect them" (Foroohar 2019, 19).

More and more tech companies are demanding taxpayer money for relocating to certain cities. Amazon, for example, now ships 67 percent of its packages to customers using Amazon delivery, tearing up local roads, and taking tax subsidies although it dodges many taxes (Vuocolo 2020).

Big Tech firms have eluded tax laws via the same methods of the early 2000s Wall Street. If they really want to help unite America, they should actually pay taxes like the thousands of small companies instead of only paying 11 to 15 percent in taxes because data and intellectual property can be offshored (Foroohar 2019, 30). And it's a substantial amount. Amazon, Facebook, Google, Netflix, Apple, and Microsoft have collectively avoided one hundred billion dollars of taxes in the last ten years (ibid.., 201). Big Tech takes billions in tax credits, subsidies, and steals what otherwise would be tax revenue for essential services including roads, libraries, and schools (Hawley 2021, 114)

Author Rana Foroohar compares Big Tech and Wall Street before the 2008 crash; its "deny and deflect" attitude, "corporate mythology, opacity, complexity, and size" (ibid.., 169). Not to mention, Facebook sells your data, uses customers as guinea pigs without telling them, and blatantly lies to reporters and the general public.

Instead of what's happening, Facebook and Twitter can manipulate what topics trend, and even Netflix claims to offer "top five" videos for that day, which they could use to promote their own content over competitors.

One former Facebook news curator said, "Facebook got a lot of pressure about not having a trending topic for Black Lives Matter." "They realized it was a problem, and they boosted it in the ordering. They gave it preference over other topics" (Hawley 2021, 98).

ALGORITHMS AND AI

In 2021, algorithms are the name of the game. They quite literally run our lives, from loans being approved, suggesting dating profiles, and even job-hunting (Stern 2021).

Algorithms are like giving a recipe to a computer: it follows the instructions to create the same output.

With a flood of data, companies are analyzing and selling data like never before. That includes, but is not limited to:

1. College recruiting

2. Credit limits

3. Netflix suggestions

4. Search engines

5. YouTube video suggestions

One common misconception of algorithms is they are less biased than a human—they are as biased—meaning skewing to certain results—as whomever wrote it. And the current tech giants like Facebook and Twitter will likely never voluntarily share that. Algorithms aren't inherently bad, but we should be cautious what we trust algorithms to determine.

In 2016 after news broke that Facebook curated its newsfeed with more liberal stories than conservative, many people were outraged. Since then, some companies including *The Wall Street Journal* have been watching Facebook closely.

Tech wizard and partner at Microsoft Wizard Danah Boyd wrote in a 2016 op-ed titled "Facebook Must Be Accountable to the Public": "What is of concern right now is not that human beings are playing a role in shaping news—they always have—it is the veneer of objectivity provided by Facebook's interface, the claims of neutrality enabled by the integration of algorithmic processes, and the assumption that what is prioritized reflects only the interests and actions of the users (the 'public sphere') and not those of Facebook, advertisers, or other powerful entities."

"There was never neutrality, and never will be..." (ibid..).

Mathematician and data scientist Cathy O'Neil explains, "I like to say that algorithms are opinions embedded in code. And that algorithms are not objective. Algorithms are optimized to some definition of success. So, if you can imagine, if a commercial enterprise builds an algorithm, to their definition of success, it's a commercial interest. It's usually profit" (O'Neil 2018).

The digital age has not come without casualties. Our lives are considerably less private while Tech companies sell that private information to companies that often have poor intentions. For example, O'Neil explains how for-profit colleges use data to target vulnerable communities. A 2012 Senate committee report described how now-shuttered, Missouri-based Vatterott College focused recruiting on "Welfare Mom w/ Kids. Pregnant Ladies. Recent Divorce. Low Self-Esteem. Low Income Jobs. Experienced a Recent Death. Physically/Mentally Abused. Recent Incarceration. Drug Rehabilitation. Dead-End Jobs. No Future."

Twenty-four hours a day in Detroit, thousands of cameras record activity at gas stations, restaurants, grocery and liquor stores, apartment buildings, churches, and schools for police to watch in real time (Detroit 2021). We've integrated technology into our daily lives to start cars remotely, turn down the thermostat from bed, and track heart rates via wearable tech, but with automation, our peace of mind has dwindled.

Yet another instance of our data being taken advantage of, a federal class-action lawsuit claims a Dallas employee of security giant ADT accessed hundreds of remote home security cameras without the authority to do so.

The lawsuit claims the employee added himself as an admin, granting unfettered live-stream access to see customers "in various states of undress" and during "moments of physical intimacy" (ibid.). This employee's actions went unnoticed for nearly seven years before finally being caught (ibid.).

Business for Big Tech companies boomed during the COVID-19 pandemic, ballooning these already massive behemoths to unfathomable sizes. While the COVID-19 pandemic bankrupted and caused many small businesses to go under, it was a steroid for Amazon and the gang. New York University Professor Scott Galloway writes in *Post Corona: From Crisis to Opportunity* that Apple worked for forty-two years to break a one trillion dollars valuation but spent only twenty weeks, from March to August 2020, to leap from one to two trillion dollars (Galloway 2020, xviii).

In 2020, five companies—Amazon, Apple, Facebook, Google, and Microsoft comprised 21 percent of the value of all publicly traded US companies, Galloway writes (ibid.).

We haven't seen this sort of consolidation of corporate power since the oil and railroad barons of the late 1800s. In many aspects, these barons controlled the flow of goods and information and it's challenging to compare it to company power today.

Facebook owns the four most downloaded apps in 2019: Facebook, Facebook Messenger, WhatsApp, and Instagram—but even more concerning, they own *all* the data associated with them. And how they use that data is largely a secret (Shead 2019).

In a Pew study, 74 percent of Facebook users say they didn't know Facebook collected their traits and interests until directed to a Facebook policy page (ibid.). A separate Pew study found that 62 percent of respondents said social networks control too much news people see (Shearer and Grieco 2019).

As public discourse pivoted online in 2020, many tech companies decided what speech they did and did not like—wiping some people off the digital Earth, even when they might be right. On May 26, 2021, Facebook said it will stop removing posts saying COVID-19 might have originated in a lab after months of removing speech (Lima 2021). I've spoken to dozens of people permanently banned from platforms for posting memes and jokes. Facebook threatened to kick The Babylon Bee, a satire site, off the platform and demonetize them after Snopes, a twenty-five-year veteran company, felt the need to debunk an article titled "CNN Purchases Industrial-Sized Washing Machine to Spin News before Publication" (Ford 2020).

Despite all the benefits that technology offers, serious concerns linger when contemplating the future of technology in our lives. The propulsion of alleged censorship will push us to ask tough questions: Should Big Tech be the arbiter of truth? Should we regulate data and algorithms? Should we ditch Big Tech for a service that doesn't sell our secrets?

CHAPTER 7

BIG POWER PROBLEMS

———

In May 2021, a second wave of COVID-19 devastated India, which had little supplemental oxygen or vaccines. On May 11, Reuters reported the rolling seven-day average death count climbed to 3,405. Residents rightly began criticizing the government, which ordered Facebook, Instagram, and Twitter to remove dozens of social media posts criticizing the government's handling of the pandemic and calling on Narendra Modi, India's prime minister, to resign. Four months prior, Modi had declared victory against COVID-19, saying India "has saved humanity from a big disaster by containing the coronavirus." In other words, the government was trying to abuse social media to hide its failure that killed an unknown number of people. Still, they were more concerned about public relations than saving lives.

India's government said the posts it targeted "spread fake or misleading information," could "incite panic and could "hinder its response to the pandemic," the *New York Times* reported on April 25, 2020. Or in University of Delhi professor Aftab Alam's opinion, "Because you know it's easier to take down tweets than it is to ensure oxygen supplies," he tweeted.

When just a few people or bodies hold most means of communication, it's easy to restrict free speech—especially when people are dying, and the government doesn't want people to know. But the real issue is power. Here are five Big Power Problems.

WHEN GOVERNMENT AND TECH COLLUDE TO CENSOR SPEECH THEY DON'T LIKE.

You might think something like this couldn't happen in America. But on July 15, 2020, President Joe Biden's press secretary Jen Psaki said:

"We're flagging problematic posts for Facebook that spread disinformation. We're working with doctors and medical experts…who are popular with their audience with accurate information," she said (Conklin 2021). "So, we're helping get trusted content out there." There's a fine line between flagging posts for Facebook's independent review and government ordering social media to silence speech, which would be a direct violation of the First Amendment.

US Rep. Thomas Massie summarized Psaki's statement well. "This is 'Ministry of Truth' level malfeasance. They're literally admitting to colluding with media to control the narrative. This is censorship. #dontflagmebro," he tweeted. "These are state-controlled-media tactics we rightfully condemn in dictatorships. If an administration has a message to get out, let them express it. But when the government works to throttle speech with which they disagree, it has crossed a line."

This is especially ironic since the US government deliberately spread misinformation early in the pandemic regarding masks. Specifically, on February 29, 2020, US Surgeon General Dr. Jerome Adams begged the general public not to buy masks in a now-deleted tweet.

"Seriously people—STOP BUYING MASKS!

They are NOT effective in preventing the general public from catching #Coronavirus, but if healthcare providers can't get them to care for sick patients, it puts them and our communities at risk!"

This was months before nearly every state enacted a mask mandate. Even now, in July 2021, Dr. Anthony Fauci, director of the National Institute of Allergy and Infectious Diseases, pushes for children and vaccinated people to wear masks (Maxie 2021).

On May 13, 2021, President Joe Biden said on C-SPAN, "Now, I want to be clear about what the CDC is saying and what the CDC is not saying. The CDC is saying they have concluded that fully vaccinated people are at a very, very low risk of getting COVID-19. Therefore, if you've been fully vaccinated, you no longer need to wear a mask. Let me repeat: If you are fully vaccinated, you no longer need to wear a mask."

However, Biden's CDC reversed that policy, so should Biden's account be terminated for spreading misinformation?

An April 7, 2021, Pew Research study says 97 percent of Americans own a cell phone in 2021—up from 35 percent in 2011. Now governments and companies use that access to spy on 97 percent of us and sell our data.

BIG POWER PROBLEMS

If these tech lords—Google, Facebook, Twitter, Instagram, Yahoo, Alphabet, and LinkedIn—conspire to wipe all reference of you off the face of the digital Earth, they pretty well can. Thousands of people have been banned or kicked off Facebook for jokes, some banished like they never existed.

This came to a head after January 6 when Twitter and Facebook banned the then-leader of the free world from reaching the most-traveled areas of the internet as much as Twitter, Facebook, YouTube, and a range of others did for former President Donald Trump.

Even after his presidency, YouTube has blocked Trump's rallies in 2021 near the border and Ohio for the 2024 election—although now he's just some seventy-five-year-old dude (Maas 2021). On April 1, 2020, *BBC* reported Facebook has banned Trump's voice from the platform, and Twitter cut the then-president off from his more than eighty-eight million followers over the January 6 clumsy attack in which five people died nearby: one was shot by Capitol Police, one died of a drug overdose, and three died from natural causes (Jansen 2021).

YouTube hasn't responded to multiple requests for comment.

Meanwhile, when the Taliban took over Afghanistan in August 2021, its official spokesperson tweeted regular updates, amassing a following of 287,000 (Halaschak 2021). So, does the Taliban, which often doesn't let women work outside the home, achieve higher education, or even drive a car, deserve to be blocked less than Trump? During the quick fall of

Afghanistan, one Taliban judge said all gay men would be stoned to death or crushed by a giant wall and that women must get a permit to leave the house (Pleasance 2021). But that's apparently not bad enough for Twitter's boot.

Since the COVID-19 pandemic, social media has facilitated most public discourse, highlighting topics and dissent that Big Tech doesn't like.

Instead of going to the bar to talk politics, we tweet, post on Facebook or on any other thousands of apps. Meeting hall posters are replaced with email Zoom invites. Many public officials have reached more constituents than ever, posting videos and responses on a medium through which people can watch it when available. Instead of heading to a city square or the state capital, we advocate policy change through social media and digital sites.

Public discourse and everyday life from paying electric bills to tollways have quickly gone digital. I've talked with some teachers who post lesson plans on websites, Zoomed with pupils' parents, and unfortunately attend "virtual" field trips.

But online, your voice, profile, and online persona can be deleted with one click—especially if they find you annoying. Private sites can permanently ban you for any reason. Moreover, they don't even have to tell you what rule you violated, which post it was, or allow you to appeal the penalty in some cases. The idea is users can vote with their fingers which apps to use, as long as one company doesn't buy multiple sites.

Despite trumpeting open and free speech, what Facebook and Twitter really mean is as long as it agrees with social media giants. Their lack of transparency shows this, where they pick and choose enforcement of their vague, undefined rules. Even though they proclaim to promote open and free speech, they really mean as long as it agrees with their narrative.

On April 9, 2021, *The Daily Caller's* Logan Hall tweeted one quick example, which I'll explore later:

"Twitter bans the sitting president

Facebook punishes anyone questioning Fauci and CDC guidance

Amazon removes conservative books

YouTube pulls DeSantis roundtable

Sensing a pattern yet?"

MARKET SHARE MONSTERS/ UNCOMPETITIVE BEHAVIOR

Tech companies now focus on retaining market share instead of innovating new goods or service. If a competitor threatens market share, they buy it. For example, Vine was the first TikTok, an app with more downloads than YouTube, Instagram, Facebook, and Snapchat according to a Failory analysis. My generation lost its mind, and Twitter noticed fast—buying the company for thirty million dollars in 2012 before it even launched (Newton 2016). But it was a flop. Vine's net worth neared a ten-million-dollar valuation but was reportedly losing ten million dollars per month as well as market share to Instagram for its fifteen-second video feature (Quittner 2017). Twitter shut down Vine in 2016–17.

Big social media companies love big government, which is why Facebook spent nearly twenty million dollars lobbying the US government in 2020 (Markup 2021). Entrenched social media companies use their capital, lobbying, and the revolving door between the two to hike regulations and drown small but star companies (Soave 2021). For years, Facebook has lobbied for updated internet regulations, which in crony-capitalism speak means they want to shut out small competitors via government (ibid.).

Facebook CEO Mark Zuckerberg wrote of these small but burgeoning companies in an email: "These businesses are nascent, but the network is established, the brands are already meaningful, and if they grow to a large scale they could be very disruptive to us" (Hawley 2021, 121). Whether these companies fend off competition via buying them out and shutting them down or hiking barriers to market entry via regulation, they're no longer a threat.

For example, Amazon advocates raising the federal minimum wage—a barrier to competition—to fifteen dollars an hour because they can afford it, and thousands of smaller competitors can't. In 2018, Google's parent company Alphabet spent nearly twenty-two million dollars lobbying (ibid.., 119). They aren't alone. In 2020, Facebook, Apple, Netflix, and Google hit all-time lobbying spending records (Reklaitis 2020).

Big Tech critics' most significant complaint boils down to power. Alphabet has bought over 200 companies ranging from Nest smart home products to DoubleClick, an ad management system, YouTube, the most-used social media site, Waze, a competitor to Google Maps and Fitbit, Inc., which tracks personal health, and Motorola Mobility (Huang 2021). The giant will likely continue to buy out any competition.

If a company rivals them, Facebook buys it—such as Instagram and WhatsApp, or in Amazon's case, Zappo. And even more, some of these companies are so ruthlessly efficient that they show how mediocre government services, like the post office, are compared to Amazon's same-day and even two-hour shipping in some locations, thanks to workers who pee in bottles and defecate in bags to rush your packages (Klippenstein 2021).

While the COVID-19 pandemic and government's response bankrupted small businesses and vulnerable companies, it acted as a steroid to Big Tech companies such as Amazon, Zoom, and others. In *Post Corona: From Crisis to Opportunity*, New York University Professor Scott Galloway writes that Apple worked for forty-two years to break a one trillion dollars valuation but spent only twenty weeks, from March to August 2020, to leap from one to two trillion dollars. Meanwhile, Tesla's valuation jumped to more than Toyota, Volkswagen, and Honda combined (Klender 2020).

In 2020, five companies—Amazon, Apple, Facebook, Google, and Microsoft comprised 21 percent of the value of all publicly traded US companies (Galloway 2020, 41). The more companies Big Tech buys, the more they control your options. If Facebook buys internet companies, can you be kicked off them completely? Currently, Facebook users can lose Oculus Virtual Reality privileges if they're kicked off the platform. A Federal Communications Commission filing by Facebook subsidiary, PointView Tech, LLC, suggests it will launch satellites into space beaming connectivity worldwide (Harris 2018).

Amazon/Jeff Bezos has bought companies rapidly in the last few decades. On May 6, 2021, author Keith Boykin tweeted:

- MGM: $8.45 billion (2021)

- Ring: $1.2 billion (2018)

- Whole Foods: $13.4 billion (2017)

- Twitch: $970 million (2014)

- Washington Post: $250 million (2013)

- Zappos: $1.2 billion (2009)

- Audible: $300 million (2008)

- IMDB: $55 million (1998)

TECH INVASION

In the last two decades, the world has drastically shifted how and where we work, travel, play, and get our news.

Facebook and Twitter *are* the mainstream media, Will Oremus writes in his OneZero newsletter on November 7, 2020.

In January 2021, Pew Research found "More than eight-in-ten US adults (86 percent) say they get news from a smartphone, computer, or tablet "often" or "sometimes," including 60 percent who say they do so often."

Facebook and YouTube's algorithms shape the minds of more than 2.2 billion people, including what stories they see, their opinions of specific political movements, and policy proposals. Algorithms determine what video content is effective. On YouTube, more than 70 percent of the views come from the recommendations, Guillaume Chaslot, a former Google engineer, told *The Wall Street Journal.*

TikTok's algorithm is even more powerful. He estimated 90 percent of TikTok videos are recommended by algorithms determined partly by how long you linger on a certain category of content—what you like and dislike (ibid.). Unfortunately, that includes negative moods such as depression and death. Pre-social media, we experienced the same terrible events, but we didn't wallow in our darkest thoughts for an undetermined amount of time. In a *WSJ* investigation that created one hundred bot TikTok accounts with certain interests, one user initially watched one or two videos about depression (ibid.). Soon after that, 93 percent of the videos shown were tagged with depression (ibid.). These actions can have large implications. Facebook has 2.2 billion global users (Statista 2021). If Facebook were a country, it would be the largest on earth.

When Cambridge Analytica scraped data from eighty-seven million Facebook users, packaged with voter records and hundreds of data points about ideological issues to allegedly swing the election for former President Donald Trump, it was the second publicly acknowledged time social media sites played a major role in a presidential election (Hern 2018). President Barack Obama's team also heavily used social media for fundraising and collecting people's data Investors.com wrote in a March 19, 2018 editorial.

In the words of Trump's 2016 digital manager Theresa Hong, "Without Facebook, we wouldn't have won" (Foroohar 2019, 233).

Most Americans now get their news through social media, apparently authorizing Twitter, YouTube, and Facebook as the arbiter of truth to decide which stories go viral and which die in darkness. YouTube pulled a video of Florida Governor Ron DeSantis, claiming his panel of doctors and epidemiologists from Oxford, Stanford, and Harvard were spreading COVID-19 misinformation (Wilson and Ross 2021). Who decides what's misinformation, and why do tech companies censor the opinions of some medical experts, while others are promoted using taxpayer money?

Facebook co-founder Chris Hughes said, "The most problematic aspect of Facebook's power is Mark [Zuckerberg's] unilateral control over speech. There is no precedent for his ability to monitor, organize, and even censor the conversations of two billion people" (Hughes 2019).

In the words of Kanye West, "No one man should have all that power."

GATEKEEPERS OF THE INTERNET: TECH-FUNDED AND INFLUENCED ELECTIONS? MY OH MY

Who chooses whose voice should be heard via social media?

Copious power to arbitrarily enforce on political enemies is concerning. For example, when Project Veritas founder James O'Keefe exposed a CNN employee for admitting they cranked COVID-19 deaths as "fear porn" and pushed other "propaganda," Twitter banned O'Keefe. Twitter says it was for violating its "platform manipulation and spam policy" (Coldewey 2021).

After decades of relatively lax standards, social media companies are starting to act as gatekeepers of the internet and its services by proxy. These tech companies were allowed to thrive under a system open and friendly to them, and now they are shutting the door behind them to limit competition. As companies grow to behemoths, we should consider how much of our lives we allow them to control and influence— where we sell, how we get internet, and talk with others. It's easy to justify doing business on Facebook because it's easy. People of all ages and political persuasions use it for Marketplace, the third largest selling spot in the world, groups to stay in touch with exciting groups of people, and funny memes. Social media and search engines can gather massive amounts of our data and influence us on a widespread, scalable platform, a power easily abused. Then, companies can divide people based only on their perceived political beliefs. Even worse, sometimes Big Tech can influence government operations.

In a CCA at Hillsdale College in November 2020, Google whistleblower Robert Epstein explained the Google search bar, seen about 500 million times a day, treats users differently depending on their politics.

"Among other things, at some point and time, we found Google's home page had a 'Go vote reminder'...We learned from the monitoring we were doing that the 'Go vote reminder' was going just to liberals," he said (ibid.).

Epstein says this strategy can shift millions of votes if continued day-after-day for months to voters of one party. Other tech companies aren't even trying to hide their influence on elections. Zuckerberg and his wife Priscella Chan, through their Chicago-based nonprofit, the Center for Technology and Civic Life (CTCL), contributed $400 million nationwide into the 2020 election with the stated goal of promoting safe and reliable voting. CTCL said the funds supported local elections, including poll worker recruitment, hazard pay, poll rentals, and nonpartisan voter education to award over 2,500 grants to city and county elections offices nationwide (ibid.).

In July of 2019, Dr. Robert Epstein told the Senate Judiciary Committee that his research revealed: "biased search results generated by Google's search algorithm likely impacted undecided voters in a way that gave at least 2.6 million votes to Hillary Clinton" in the 2016 presidential election. He also voted for Clinton. He alleged Big Tech collusion could swing mass numbers of votes—enough to influence an election (ibid.).

In 2019, Epstein testified in front of Congress that Big Tech should be watched closely in 2020 (ibid..). If these companies all support the same candidate, he said they could likely shift upwards of fifteen million votes to that candidate with no one knowing and without a paper trail (ibid.).

Epstein's testimony claimed that "Google presents a serious threat to democracy and human autonomy" (ibid..). According to his research findings, "Google has likely been determining the outcomes of upwards of 25 percent of the national elections worldwide since at least 2015" and "in the weeks leading up to the 2018 election, bias in Google's search results may have shifted upwards of 78.2 million votes to the candidates of one political party" (ibid..).

Over time, that can shift millions of votes, Epstein says, which may have contributed to a record number of people voting. Facebook has been shoving money into academic research proving they can influence their millions of users (ibid..).

Overall, Epstein explained the Google platform like this: If the name accurately explained what it did, it'd be "'Google Surveillance and Advertising' because surveillance is what they do. All of these platforms you use like Gmail, Google Docs, they are surveillance platforms; that's all they are from a business perspective...You're being tricked into giving away massive amounts of personal information, which the company then monetizes" (ibid..).

Can a third-party group fund public services? Should it? This is just one problem we'll face in the future.

BIG PROBLEMS, BIG SOLUTIONS

Tech not only brings us incredible new solutions but also massive problems. Should Facebook and Google be regulated since both's reach could affect the outcome of a presidential election? Or would government regulation exacerbate the problem? Most Americans now get their news through social media, which has sparked Twitter and Facebook to become the arbiter of truth in which stories go viral and which ones die in darkness.

It's a race to the moon for Amazon, Facebook, Tesla, and a range of tech companies with cash to burn. SpaceX's plan for a global satellite internet service, Starlink, was recently approved by the FCC to perform similar work as PointView Tech's plans (Greig 2018). Starlink plans to launch thousands of satellites in LEO. Richard Branson-backed OneWeb is also planning its satellite internet service, its website says. And soon, Amazon? (Will they offer two-day shipping from planet to planet?)

Amazon filed its first papers with the US government for approval to launch a network of 3,236 satellites through a subsidiary called Kuiper Systems LLC to provide high-speed internet service (Boyle 2019). The race to commercialize space launched long ago, but one winner could be the 3.8 billion people worldwide that don't currently have access to high-speed internet, and by proxy, an opportunity for a better life. Alphabet has made significant strides with Google Fiber, as has SpaceX and Facebook with satellite-based internet, TechRepublic reported in 2017. Still, how much power are you willing to give one company? What happens when Amazon and Facebook take over and monetize space travel?

In "The information trade: How Big Tech conquers countries, challenges our rights, and transforms our world," tech writer Alexis Wichowski coined the term "net states" to describe these entities that she says are out "to change the world—not just in theory, but in defense, diplomacy, public infrastructure, and citizen servers" (p. 5).

Google Ventures's website says it invests in companies "across all stages and sectors, with a focus on enterprise, life sciences, consumer, and frontier technology."

"We're drawn to founders who push the edge of what's possible. Our investments span the technology stack, from applications to infrastructure, and across the enterprise spectrum from developer operations to security, data platforms, and beyond" (ibid..).

That includes fintech, healthcare, pharmacies, medicine, and government. Massive companies frequently crash and burn, no matter their current market position. We shouldn't tie the internet structure of quality to select private companies that can deny the service to customers or bail out Big Tech in the future.

CHAPTER 8

THE ONLINE GENERATIONS

When former President Donald Trump's supporters broke into the United States Capitol on January 6, many of the trespassers criminally implicated themselves via social media and GPS data.

In a defense attorney's worst nightmare, former West Virginia lawmaker Derrick Evans filmed himself trespassing into the Capitol. Court documents say three minutes and fifty-six seconds into the video he states, "We're in, we're in! Derrick EVANS is in the Capitol!" This is just one example of how we've moved our lives onto the digital sphere in the last decade. We post onto social media pictures of our apartments, our significant others, and family deaths or job promotions.

And younger generations are more comfortable sharing normal private moments—births, deaths, and everything in between—for the world to see.

If my parents saw the tweets that go viral on Twitter, they'd probably be shocked about the level of intimacy and vulnerability thrown onto social media for the whole world to see, depending on privacy settings. But often, parents are busy with a career and children and friends and the rush of daily life and are either unaware or uninterested with how and what kids do with their screen time. Raising a kid between the ages of twelve through eighteen is a full-time job.

Many families grow up documenting children's accomplishments and failures online. But should we introduce minors to the world—possibly naked in a bathtub? While some moments are precious and you may want to share with friends and family, the consequences of an always-on generation are rearing its head.

Adults are liable for their actions, but for kids with undeveloped brains, the internet can be a scary place. The permanence of social media means that kids can tweet dumb things that ruin their lives later. A single bad take, Instagram post, or OnlyFans account can get you kicked out of medical school or blacklisted from your dream company.

When Kimberly Diei, a University of Tennessee pharmacy graduate student, posted pictures of her scantily clad body on Twitter and Instagram under a pseudonym account of "kimmykasi," she said she was just having fun (Hartocollis 2021). Diei racked up more than 19,500 followers on IG and 2,000 on Twitter before someone snitched multiple times to the university, which initially ordered her expelled in September of 2020 for "vulgar" posts before reversing the decision (ibid.). Diei filed a federal lawsuit to clarify the blurry boundaries between public and private life in online speech.

If Diei walked into class at UT nearly naked, that might be grounds for expulsion. But can universities control what students say online, especially under a fake account unassociated with the institution?

If a 2021 US Supreme Court decision *Mahanoy Area School District v. B.L* is any indication, schools can shove off gagging online student speech. The Supreme Court ruled eight to one that a Pennsylvania school violated the First Amendment by punishing a student who sent images of her and a friend flipping off the camera to about 250 Snapchat friends regarding "school," "softball," "cheer," and "everything" while outside school grounds after not making the cheerleading squad.

While some might jump to conclusions, what the girl's Snapchat didn't show was context. The girl, who was a minor, could have just been dumped by a significant other, wrecked her car the same day, or failed a test. All of us have likely had a rough day and shouted something we regretted, flipped off a car that cut us off, or lashed out without reason. Our mistake just wasn't highlighted by the nation's top court for everyone to see. To me, that sounds like the girl had a rough day, but nothing worth punishment. Free speech includes speech you don't like.

Our online actions have more consequences than ever, Kate Eichhorn writes.

"Until the end of the twentieth century, most young people could take one thing for granted: their embarrassing behavior would eventually be forgotten. It might be a bad haircut, or it might be getting drunk and throwing up at a party, but in an analog era, even if faux pas were documented in a photograph, the likelihood of its being reproduced and widely circulated for years was minimal. The same held true for stupid or offensive remarks. Once you went off to college, there was no reason to assume that embarrassing moments from your high school years would ever resurface.

Not anymore. Today, people enter adulthood with much of their childhood and adolescence still up for scrutiny" (Eichhorn 2019).

University of Rochester Medical Center research says many brains don't fully develop until age twenty-five. If our legal system treats kids as having undeveloped brains, should we let those undeveloped brains roam wild in unchartered territories? That's a decision best left up to the parents, but kids should be proficient with technology as it will likely consume and transform the future of work.

It's a terrifying time to raise children with more things to worry about than ever before—diseases, child obesity, and bad influences. For the first time, we're seeing millennials grow up constantly connected to the internet, meaning that one-time stupid mistakes might never be forgotten.

When you think about sex offenders, you probably think about a creepy old man who rarely leaves the basement. But if we dive into the data, you'll find a different reality. As Reason's Robby Soave writes in "*Tech Panic: Why We Shouldn't Fear Facebook and the Future*," the most common age for sex offenders is fourteen.

Finding love is hard, but finding it when you're a confused, horny teenager seems impossible. I don't have kids yet, but I know friends and family who tell me nightmare situations where kids send nude pictures, which if acquired by law enforcement, could derail their life before they even got a chance to succeed.

Even if two teenagers consensually send naked pictures, they could both be charged as sex offenders. Thankfully, Snapchat's transient properties aim to prevent these pictures, but loopholes like screenshots or photographing a Snapchat still exist.

Moreover, what society deems as acceptable is rapidly changing. Personalities are being canceled for things they did or said fifteen to thirty years ago—which is utterly wild. The permanence of social media means people get insulted and attacked for changing their minds on a topic, even though you should change your mind when weighing new information. Even former President Barack Obama changed his mind on opposing gay marriage (Steinmetz 2015).

Would you want to be friends with someone who can't admit they're wrong and made a mistake? Changing your mind isn't a weakness. It means you're human.

MODERN PRIVACY EXPECTATIONS

I was born in 1995 and am likely the last generation that didn't grow up online (or the option to be online).

For me as a child, "fun" was crawling around in the woods, bluffs, and lakes in Southern Illinois, riding four-wheelers, and shooting guns (supervised and well-trained). Nobody tracked me or my siblings, and we learned personal responsibility through minor injuries and mistakes. I doubt many companies in the 2000s wanted to buy my data. But for many urban families, kids now explore online, playing games, watching movies, and more. This stream of constant data is bought and sold by the government, companies, and even used to create online profiles that could lead to a scary future.

Whenever you buy items from a retailer, it tracks those items via your credit card, guest ID number, or name and can sell that data to interested parties. Some places are scary-good at data mining, like how Target discovered a high-schooler was pregnant before her parents did by analyzing purchase data (Hill 2012).

In the modern era, social media and what you post online can get you fired, divorced, charged with violating parole, or thrown into prison.

Wherever you go in some cities, somebody is watching. Whether it's cameras equipped with facial recognition, the company that's buying your Mastercard purchase data, or the government nabbing your plates via an automated license plate reader, our privacy is eroding.

In the words of Robert Scheer's "They Know Everything About You," "Privacy is a matter of individual choice as to what to reveal about one's behavior to others." (preface x).

In November 2018, Pew Research found that about 72 percent of Americans report feeling that all or most of what they do online is being tracked by advertisers and most Americans feel it's impossible to live without having data collected by the government. Close to half of adults believe at least most of their online activities are being tracked by the government. Nearly 80 percent of Americans say they are concerned with the way companies use their data, while 64 percent are concerned with government data use (ibid.).

America was founded upon the belief that one is considered innocent until proven guilty—that the burden of proof is on the prosecutor—but that idea is being chipped away as law enforcement can now skirt Fourth Amendment requirements and buy people's personal data and use "predictive" policing that often violates the Freedom of Association.

There's more data available about people than ever before—the highways people frequent, captured by automated license plate readers, where you shop and hang out, captured by facial recognition, and patterns of where you spend your time, seen through cell phone data and live-stream cameras in over 700 private Detroit businesses that provide twenty-four-seven live stream feed to the Detroit Police Department.

Even "anonymous" data can expose your identity.

A December 2018 *New York Times* investigation analyzed "anonymous" data and easily discovered the cell phone user's identity. For one woman, apps "recorded her whereabouts as often as every two seconds," the *Times* wrote. That's because our identities are derived from how and where we spend our time—where we work, where our kids learn, and where we go to let loose and relax. "In about four months of data reviewed by the *Times*, her location was recorded over 8,600 times—on average, once every twenty-one minutes," the article notes (ibid.). Not only that, but researchers at Microsoft found that location data can be used to predict future locations. "While your location in the distant future is in general highly independent of your recent location, it is likely to be a good predictor of your location exactly one week from now."

This might seem strange at first, but much of our tech does this. When I schedule a trip to Denver or Miami, my phone notifies me of things to do there. Depending on your Google Maps settings, sometimes a phone notifies you of the commute time to the gym or church or school. A 2013 study published in Nature.com analyzing 1.5 million people's mobility over fifteen months found that human movement is unique–with a handful of data points, they could identify, 95 percent of the time, an individual just based on movement.

"In fact, in a dataset where the location of an individual is specified hourly and with a spatial resolution equal to that given by the carrier's antennas, four spatio-temporal points are enough to uniquely identify 95 percent of the individuals," the study said.

A minute glance at a LinkedIn profile shows where you went to school, who you've worked with, and peer into your network. My LinkedIn provides my email, employer, and nearly 12,000 connections. That can be used to help someone find a great job across the country or to profile someone.

In the EU, their General Data Protection Regulation (GDPR) allows the right to be forgotten. Article 17 of the GDPR states,

"The data subject shall have the right to obtain from the controller the erasure of personal data concerning him or her without undue delay and the controller shall have the obligation to erase personal data without undue delay" if one of a number of conditions applies. "Undue delay" is considered to be about a month (ibid.).

In 2009, Askan Soltani published a KnowPrivacy study that discovered three key findings:

- Users are concerned about data collection and want greater control of their personal information (access, edit, delete).

- Users lack awareness of some data collection practices.

- Users don't know where to file their complaints.

In 2003, Joseph Turow found that 94 percent of his sample of 1,200 American adults agreed or agreed strongly with the statement, "I should have a legal right to know everything that a website knows about me."

Tech is a tool. The late Supreme Court Justice Ruth Bader Ginsburg raised a warning flag in a dissent of *Herring v. United States.*

"Inaccuracies in expansive, interconnected collections of electronic information raise grave concerns for individual liberty," she wrote. "The offense to the dignity of the citizen who is arrested, handcuffed, and searched on a public street simply because some bureaucrat has failed to maintain an accurate computer data base is evocative of the use of general warrants that so outraged the authors of the Bill of Rights" (ibid..).

Arthur Rizer, the then-director of Criminal Justice & Civil Liberties at the R Street Institute, says the amount of data tech companies and law enforcement gather is a threat to the presumption of innocence. For example, just because law enforcement can see who you're associated with on social media or pick up your phone's metadata at a particular protest, they might pursue charges or conduct surveillance they otherwise wouldn't. Rizer said that electronic data can then be used to request a Title III of the Omnibus Crime Control and Safe Streets Act of 1968—also known as the Wiretap Act.

"For a very long time the feds have 'dirtied' phone numbers by just looking at who called you and who you called and then who that number called or received calls from (and then rinsed and repeated)," Rizer said. "They would use that as circumstantial evidence that you are 'dirty' too and get Title 3s—I think the same thing is happening with social media."

Is someone deemed a criminal because they live with or are friends with ex-convicts? What if they meet up with them at a coffee shop? What if he's your best friend? What if you work or volunteer at a drug recovery center?

According to the National Conference of State Legislatures, roughly seventy-seven million Americans, or one in three adults, have a criminal record.

Technology is a tool that can be used for good or evil. Drones can be used to spy and collect private data, and can also equipped with infrared sensors to find lost hikers in the woods where other vehicles can't travel. They can deliver life-saving medicine faster than by car or perform an NFL halftime show.

Fast-forward ten years.

In an article for the Brookings Institution, University of California, Berkeley Law Professor Orin S. Kerr tells a fictional account of 2030 in which the government enacted a widespread federal surveillance system to stop terrorism—dubbed the "Minding Our National-Interest Transit or Rail" or MONITOR program.

But since there weren't stringent limits enacted on what data collected could be used for, the government sees it as a panacea for all problems: from stopping homeless people from sleeping on trains to nabbing turnstile-jumpers to figuring out the daily commute of attractive, innocent residents, and figuring out where they live and work.

Once the information is created there will be pressures to use it for a wider and wider range of government interests and a broader range of crimes. The fictional account is quickly becoming reality if residents don't pay attention and halt government's growing power.

The government never willingly reduces its power. That's why the alphabet soup of agencies goes on billion-dollar spending sprees with hard-earned taxpayer money because they believe their budgets will be slashed if they don't spend all their money.

Therefore, when the government can conduct mass surveillance, they'll use it for whatever purpose they please—spying on exes, busting teenagers smoking marijuana, or blackmailing politicians.

Riana Pfefferkorn, a cybersecurity expert at the Stanford Center for Internet and Society, called government electronic surveillance "the greatest threat to privacy in the future, aided by the private sector's collection of vast amounts of data."

Pfefferkorn pointed to China's surveillance state as where we're headed, noting the government already skirts legal process for obtaining people's data by simply purchasing it from third-party data brokers.

Pfefferkorn called for federal legislative proposals to rein in skirting apparent Fourth Amendment violations and "that allows meaningful opt-in consent (rather than the quote-un-quote 'consent' we now give in America through stuff like terms of use) and meaningful data deletion rights," Pfefferkorn said.

"That scheme, however, has to also include the third-party data broker entities, credit bureaus, etc. that hold huge amounts of data about us *without* our ever interacting with them directly or consenting to their information-gathering. As you note, however, any legislative proposal that favors protecting people's privacy by limiting private-sector acquisition of user data will come into tension with law enforcement objectives, as law enforcement agencies have become accustomed to a vast treasure trove of data held by tech companies and will surely balk at any legislative measure that might yank away any part of that windfall."

Pfefferkorn advocated to "tamp down" on burgeoning and all-encompassing electronic surveillance—ranging from license plate readers to pervasive location tracking, smart cities, facial recognition, and more that will further degrade our ability to move about anonymously in public.

Pfefferkorn suggested lawmakers might need to overrule the longstanding court precedent that you can't expect privacy when you're in public since you're voluntarily exposing your face and your movements. The precedent predates current all-encompassing surveillance technology.

"However, that is a relic of an era before automated license plate readers, body-worn police cameras, and networks of surveillance cameras installed on private premises by neighborhood associations that will then hand over footage to police," Pfefferkorn said. "And that's not to mention the troves of historical location data held by our cell phone providers, the apps we use, and our phones themselves, all of which have created a sort of 'time machine' allowing investigators to accurately summon up a thorough picture of someone's movements and activities in the past, well before they became investigative targets."

Pre-technology, surveillance was resource-intensive. Cops had to post up in grueling overnight stakeouts, struggling to stay awake. Now, we enact live stream surveillance inside our homes, while government and private companies track us outside the home as well.

"It is no longer the case that our movements in public are ephemeral or that large amounts of police resources would have to be devoted to exhaustively tracking someone's movements at all times, which in past eras had enabled a sort of 'privacy by obscurity.' We're seeing some recognition of the need to protect privacy in the pervasively surveilled age, for example in the Supreme Court's 2018 *Carpenter* decision, which rejected the contention that by moving about in public, we voluntarily give up all privacy," Pfefferkorn wrote. "But this issue, of inadequate legal protections for people's privacy expectations in public, is one that simply has to change in the future."

For example, police surveillance center in Jackson, Mississippi, will be conducting a forty-five-day pilot program to live stream the security cameras, including Amazon Ring cameras, of participating residents (Wakefiled 2020).

War company Raytheon created a technology called Rapid Information Overlay Technology (RIOT) that climbs through social media to track and even predict a person's future movement.

Phones don't only track where you are physically, but where you spend time surfing the web, and what you post on social media—and if used correctly, can become a market for obtaining personal information frequently used for recovery password questions.

"Facebook surveys" of questions to get to know you, such as your mother's maiden name, the make of your first kind of car, pet's name, and hometown.

The ushering into the digital age comes the outpouring of personal information into the public sphere. For hackers, it's just a matter to discreetly obtain personal information to hack into bank statements, 401(k) plans, and other sensitive information.

But government surveillance flips the script: People are supposed to hold the government accountable for corrupt acts because absolute power corrupts absolutely.

CHAPTER 9

CREEPY TECH AND ITS SLAYERS

———

On a sunny Saturday morning in their Dallas, Texas home, Shana Doty could be found making pancakes, playing baseball outside with her husband and son, or getting intimate in the bedroom with her husband (Hurtibise 2020). Like six million other customers in the nation, the family installed ADT Pulse to feel safer and protect the young family against evil people (ibid.). The technology let them lock doors remotely, change the thermostat, turn off lights, and live stream housewide cameras (ibid.).

Despite their precautions, a bad person exploited the technology for perverted reasons. A disgruntled, horny former ADT technician added himself as an admin to 220 accounts in the Dallas area, watching them more than 9,600 times, some for up to seven years (Oliveria 2021). Alexia Preddy was a teenager when her security technician granted himself remote access to her account. Then he accessed it nearly one hundred times to spy on her, her son and husband and other members "in their most private and intimate moments," and "for an unknown amount of time" (Hurtibise 2020).

"Moments once believed to be private and inside the sanctity of the home are now voyeuristic entertainment for a third party," the lawsuit says. "And worse, those moments could have been captured, shared with others, or even posted to the internet" (ibid..).

Preddy and Doty are lead plaintiffs in class-action lawsuits expecting hundreds of other victims to join. ADT serves more than six million customers who spent their hard-earned money on home security systems that allowed a creepy guest to spend up to seven years watching intimate life moments (ibid.). Each of the two lawsuits seeks more than five million dollars (ibid..).

Privacy lawsuits are a relatively new concept since it can be hard to prove injury or physical harm, but the exposure of privacy can hurt an infinite amount, like if the former ADT technician took pictures or videos of customers having sex and posted the video online, where it would likely live forever and tarnish their reputation. What would be a proper settlement?

Emergent questions like these are what Chicago privacy lawyer Jay Edelson has spent decades considering. Early on, Edelson knew that Silicon Valley was betting billions that they could monetize people's personal data. Edelson is one of the nation's leading plaintiff lawyers. His firm has secured over three billion dollars in settlements and verdicts for his clients while serving as lead counsel. He is also widely regarded as the top consumer privacy attorney in America, with him and his firm holding records for the largest trial verdict in a consumer privacy case ($925 million), the largest consumer privacy settlement ($650 million), and the largest TCPA settlement ($76 million). Dubbed "the most hated person in Silicon Valley" by the *New York Times*, Edelson made his name suing tech companies for privacy violations (Dougherty 2015). In three months, Edelson wrangled a record $650 million settlement from Facebook in a biometric privacy lawsuit, complicated a planned ninety-two-million-dollar settlement with TikTok, and set his sights on Clearview AI and ADT—the largest home security firm in America (Thomas 2021).

When a new product comes out, Edelson says it takes about five years until problems are found, and home security was no different. He found vulnerabilities in home security companies across the country. "It's not just ADT," Edelson said. "It's across the board."

"To us, it's one of the worst abuses when you're buying something so that you can have security, and exactly the opposite happens—you're exploited," he said. "To us, it hammers home why privacy is so important."

More and more Americans are using technology to achieve a semblance of peace of mind to protect their kids from creeps. Edelson's eyed biometrics and geolocation as battlegrounds for privacy rights, especially as our devices know more and more about us—including those controlled by employers.

Brookings Senior Fellow Darrell West explains in "How Employers Use Technology to Surveil Employees," how the switch to virtual work opened a door for employers to spy on us and learn things that is none of their business (West

2021). For example, Lisa Rene worked at an Indianapolis company operated by G. F. Fishers that installed keylogger software on her work computer without notifying employees (ibid.). The program sent information Rene typed on her computer, including passwords to her bank and personal email, to her supervisor, who allegedly looked through her financial accounts and emails (ibid.). Once Rene found out and confronted an employee, she was fired for "poor performance" (ibid..).

For many, working from home was a joke before the COVID-19 pandemic. I've worked remotely in part-or-fulltime jobs for about eight years, and people used to look at me dumbfounded when they asked where I worked daily. But some governments issued emergency COVID-19 pandemic orders legally barring in-person office work so most people were thrust into an experiment of remote work. The move left companies scrambling to control shrinkage—the financial allowance expected for lost business earnings via waste or theft. Previously, I've worked as a financial analyst where my job was to identify waste, and I was shocked at how much there was. In-person work means that your boss can monitor your work because researchers estimate that "cyberloafing" accounts for about 30 percent to 65 percent of internet usage at work, one 2011 study found. But when working remotely, nothing stops you from binge-watching *Ozarks* on Netflix while you shake your mouse in case someone's checking your activity.

So, companies bought a plethora of programs to watch employees, ranging from ActivTrak, InterGuard, Veriato 360, Teramind, WorkSmart, and Work Examiner—all surveillance tools that monitor employees' online activities, analyze data, and track keystrokes (Sevilla 2020). Some apps take screenshots every ten minutes, including anything onscreen, even if it's personal Zoom calls, texts to your wife, bank and investment information, or Amazon orders (ibid.). West digs into the barrage of methods your employer can surveil you when you work from home: from taking video surveillance to biometric attention tracking to productivity data and browser use (West 2021).

Of course, you should be working when you're on the clock. But this new tech could allow employers to obtain your passwords, bank statements, and so much more that is none of their business. COVID-19 blurred the line of how much your employer knows about you: how many pets you have, the gender of your significant other, and the iconic poster of rappers Snoop Dogg and Tupac directly behind your desk. Edelson said he's heard of many employers using this technology.

Edelson pointed out the at-will relationship between an employer and an employee—they have the authority to surveil employees to a certain extent. At issue is when employers don't tell employees that they're being tracked in scary ways like activating computer cameras, microphones, or even tracking keystrokes.

"That, in our view, is insane," Edelson said. "If you tell people to work because we have a camera on you, that's one thing. But that's not what's happening."

Edelson said the key to most privacy lawsuits is that actions are done surreptitiously. "If companies are disclosing what's going on, in almost all cases, there's no privacy suit there. It's the fact that they're hiding it."

There's a mirrored issue in social media companies handing out "community violations" that we'll discuss later and companies spying on their employees: a private company can set up cameras and log keystrokes, but the rules should be clearly stated and enforced equally, unlike Facebook's rule enforcement that whitelisted celebrities.

While some believe the solution to this challenge is strong federal privacy laws, Edelson is skeptical. A federal privacy statute has been debated since former President Barack Obama, but competing interests pull in opposite directions. In 2019, Facebook spent $16.7 million on lobbying, a 32 percent increase year to date, while Amazon spent $16.1 million (+14 percent) and Apple spent $7.4 million (+10 percent) (Feiner 2020).

Even more so, the lobbyists are extremely good at their job and act like laws passed actually accomplish what their names say.

"Often the statutes are written by the industries that are being regulated, so they tend to have very strong names, but what they end up doing is gutting state law, and having a very weak federal statute that doesn't really allow for any meaningful enforcement," Edelson said.

Even when some privacy suits had success, the penalties have been minuscule, Edelson said. For example, Google and YouTube agreed to pay $170 million and implement special provisions for videos targeting children according to an FTC press release (Brandom 2020) (Kelly 2019). The FTC handed

Facebook a five-billion-dollar fine—the largest US tech company fine so far over Cambridge Analytica violations on Facebook (Kelly 2019). Edelson says the fines aren't proportional to the violation and the system is broken. Many plaintiffs' attorneys take very bad deals where very little goes to the class, Edelson told me. "To me, this is the biggest threat to our privacy rights," Edelson said. "You have these enormous privacy violations, and there are just slaps on the wrist."

One solution is to give tech companies skin in the game, whether that's stupendous payouts for screwups or another reason they won't abuse their power, as author Nassim Talib explains.

"I'm making a ton of money by ripping people's privacy rights away, and maybe I get caught 10 percent of the time, and then I'll spend ten million dollars, which isn't a big deal to these companies that are making hundreds of millions, billions of dollars," Edelson said.

One somewhat terrifying example is Clearview AI. Imagine you're at the bar with your friends when you notice a cute girl sitting alone on the other side. But instead of talking to her, you snap a picture, save it into an app that pulls public photos along with links of exactly who she is, likely where she works, and who her friends are, and possibly what city in which she lives. Welcome to Clearview AI, a database of over three billion images of people scraped across the internet (Valinsky 2019). That's 4.6 times the number of images in the FBI's database (Hill 2020). Clearview's database size significantly exceeds that of others used by law enforcement and is more accurate since it illegally scraped photos we regularly upload to YouTube, Facebook, and even Venmo—violating their terms of service (ibid.). It has been sold to banks, private individuals, the Department of Justice, and retailers such as Best Buy, although now it's limited to government entities (Mac 2020). More than 600 law enforcement agencies have adopted Clearview technology in the past year alone (Hill 2020).

Often to companies this big, the revenue model is a feature instead of a bug because "There's almost no fine that would matter to them because if they had to follow the law, they wouldn't have a business," Edelson told me.

Civil liberty advocates worry Clearview AI is ripe for abuse.

"Unbeknownst to the public, this company has offered up this massive faceprint database to private companies, police, federal agencies, and wealthy individuals, allowing them to secretly track and target whomever they wished using face recognition technology," wrote ACLU attorney Nathan Freed Wessler on May 28, 2020. "That company is Clearview AI, and it will end privacy as we know it if it isn't stopped."

"If allowed, Clearview will destroy our rights to anonymity and privacy—and the safety and security that both bring," Wessler writes. "People can change their names and addresses to shield their whereabouts and identities from individuals who seek to harm them, but they can't change their faces" (Wessler 2020).

Tech companies are worth so much because they are good at predicting and forming the future. "The future that they are building is one where we're being tracked all the time," Edelson said. "If you look at Facebook's model and other companies that are employing Facial recognition technology, first what they want to do is figure out what you're doing online, and then they want to see if that translates to the real world."

"So say I'm searching for XYZ, maybe some sneakers, and then I'm going to a mall and I'm trying on sneakers." Companies are getting better at getting that information through more creative means.

In 2018, Google reportedly bought Mastercard data to build a tool for advertisers to discover whether and how often online advertisements translated into an in-store purchase (Liao 2018).

Many malls have camera-equipped mannequins to reduce theft and get customer data so they can check conversion rates of online customers who've visited their website and match with their online history and the exact products customers looked at online versus in-store (Stern 2012).

"The goal is not just to track what I'm doing but also to influence it," Edelson said. "Facebook has spent so much money on academic research to try to figure out how to push people in certain directions."

Facebook has been shoving money into academic research proving they can influence their millions of users—their mood, where they shop, and much more.

In a 2014 study published in the Proceedings of the National Academy of Sciences of the United States of America, researchers experimented with using Facebook users like guinea pigs, testing whether showing them negative and positive content would influence users' overall mood. They found that the feed content shown to users significantly impacts mood.

"We show, via a massive ($N = 689{,}003$) experiment on Facebook, that emotional states can be transferred to others via emotional contagion, leading people to experience the same emotions without their awareness," researchers wrote. "We provide experimental evidence that emotional contagion occurs without direct interaction between people (exposure to a friend expressing an emotion is sufficient), and in the complete absence of nonverbal cues (ibid.).

Facebook feeds content to make people happier or sadder, to visit certain retail establishments, or even to get people to vote. On July 13, 2016, The *Financial Times* reported that *Pokémon Go* used sponsored locations as a revenue source by placing in-game incentives at business locations and merged mass behavioral modification with advertising.

Businesses from McDonald's to Starbucks paid for "footfall" to their establishments on a "cost per visit" basis, just as online advertisers pay for "cost per click" (ibid.). The game engineers learned how to herd people through their towns and cities to destinations that contribute profits, all of it without game players' knowledge.

Walmart has patented technology that would enable cameras to capture shoppers' facial expressions while in the checkout lines so it could measure levels of dissatisfaction to finetune their in-store displays and real-time promotions while also localizing the pain points causing those pained looks (O'Shea 2017).

Your data is a cash cow—that's why even your calculator app wants to access location data. On a larger scale, Edelson worries this will result in large companies influencing customers' actions. One of the overarching problems with this all-encompassing surveillance is that it changes our behavior.

"We certainly would start making a lot of different decisions. People aren't going to go to that [Alcoholics Anonymous] meeting if they think now it's going to be logged," Edelson said. "They might not go to certain places of worship if that's going to be logged. They might not go to certain protests, which is already happening right now."

If you know you're being watched, will you still head to a gay bar on Saturday night, or for the sake of hiding your sexuality, bite your lip and go to a straight bar you abhor?

Technology is an incredible tool that can provide peace of mind or expose our deepest secrets. We should be vigilant and toss any tech that creeps us out to take back our privacy.

CHAPTER 10

BULLSHIT BANNING?

In 2020, you can die a digital death if a tech company chooses. First, it was Alex Jones and many other colorful figures deemed as crazy or incendiary characters who were banned by Facebook, YouTube, and Apple in 2018 (Coastan 2018). Then it escalated to the then-sitting president of the United States Donald Trump, whose presence Twitter and Facebook and YouTube continue to gag, citing his alleged encouragement of the January 6 attack on the national Capitol (Lima 2021). I have no doubt Trump would have live-tweeted the fall of Afghanistan in August 2021.

As more of the world moves online, tech companies have begun banning more and more accounts, which they can do as private companies. In six months of 2020, Twitter suspended 925,000 accounts for rule violations (Luca 2021). But often there's a good reason for the ban. For example, on November 6, 2020, CNN reported that Twitter permanently banned White House chief strategist Steve Bannon after he suggested Dr. Anthony Fauci and FBI Director Christopher Wray should be beheaded. Similarly, Facebook has blacklisted over 4,000 people and groups it associates with terrorism, hate groups, or criminal organizations (Biddle 2021).

I think few people have a problem with private companies kicking off terrorists and annoying people from their sites. But the real problem behind tech companies banning and censoring people is that companies give vague reasons for banning individual users that often seem arbitrary. Often, Facebook, Twitter, or TikTok won't even show the post or comment for which you or an entire group is kicked off.

When COVID-19 struck Michigan in March 2020, Governor Gretchen Whitmer took far-reaching actions to slow the spread. Whitmer banned paid contractors from working, closed gyms, and shuttered in-person work at many businesses and schools (McClallen 2020).

So angry Michiganders gathered in a Facebook group called "Michiganders Against Excessive Quarantine," founded by 2022 gubernatorial GOP challenger Garrett Soldano, which grew to nearly 400,000 members who opposed such widespread action (McClallen 2020).

In May 2020, Facebook shuttered the group (ibid.). Soldano said the reason was that he attended a rally of barber Karl Manke who flouted Whitmer's COVID-19 orders closing barbershops and was later fined $9,000 (ibid..). A Facebook spokesperson told me the group repeatedly violated Facebook's Community Standards. After more than five email exchanges, I was no closer to learning the reason for which the group was booted. The problem is that those standards are so vague that they mean nothing. Unless you have leaked internal company documents or a whistleblower, a reporter talking to a Facebook spokesperson is similar to talking to a brick wall.

Days prior, Facebook kicked off a nearly 10,000-person group called "Michigan United for Liberty" likely for planning multiple in-person protests at the Capitol with few social distancing and masks. (ibid..).

The spokesperson told me, "Unless government prohibits the event during this time, we allow it to be organized on Facebook. For this same reason, events that defy government's guidance on social distancing aren't allowed on Facebook."

So that means as long as the Facebook Group's event page claims that it will be social-distanced, the group is allowed, even if it's not actually following those same standards. Nice. Or the *Detroit Metro Times* reported the group's users threatened public officials—an understandable reason to dissolve a page. But Facebook wouldn't answer whether they banned the page for threatening real violence or because they wouldn't follow the six-foot social distancing rule, which former Food and Drug Administration Commissioner Dr. Scott Gottlieb later admitted was "arbitrary" (Dangor 2021). MUFL denied that group members threatened government officials, but thanks to Facebook operating as a wizard behind the curtain, we might never know (McClallen 2020).

When social media companies ban people, often it's for arbitrarily enforced reasons that equate to discrimination of ideas of people they don't like, hidden by vague, meaningless sayings such as "violating community standards," spreading "misinformation," or a range of other reasons disguised for partisan purposes according to over a year of interviews and research.

But sometimes, social media companies want to control what stories go viral and throttle reporters or stories. The real concern with social media is companies' inherent bias and the broad guidelines they selectively enforce. For example, Facebook and Twitter suppressed the *New York Post*'s story about Hunter Biden, until several months later, when the government confirmed the accusation, and other media acted like it was breaking news (Paul 2020).

Don't get me wrong; social media companies are private and can do whatever they please on their own site. But their actions to silence dissenting opinions, even of wacky conspiracy theorists, have an adverse effect to shove those who feel they don't have a voice deeper into radicalized and toxic communities. That means Alex Jones should be able to shout on Facebook about the government using chemicals that apparently turn the frogs gay. If you don't like someone, you can individually block them.

In *The Coddling of the American Mind*, First Amendment expert Greg Lukianoff and social psychologist Jonathan Haidt explain three ideas newly engrained onto younger generations: "What doesn't kill you makes you weaker; always trust your feelings, and life is a battle between good people and evil people" (p. iv). I believe this mindset that feelings are the final determinant of action, that insults and mean words can make us physically weaker, and that life is always a good-versus-evil battle has spilled into our online interactions, for the worst. Now, people on Twitter act like they are the final barrier standing between a full-blown civil war.

We should grow thicker skin and care less about what people say about us on Twitter. In the words of Dave Chapelle's Netflix special *The Closer* talking about Twitter users lodging complaints against him, he responded, "I don't give a fuck because Twitter isn't a real place."

If you see a post online you disagree with, you can ignore it instead of expending additional energy arguing online. If you can't use critical thinking skills to decipher the truth of statements, you're in for a rough ride.

Robby Soave is an editor at Reason who covers free speech and is the author of *Tech Panic*. He's named on the 2016 *Forbes* 30 Under 30 for Law and Policy. He says one risk of pushing fringe actors off Parler and the public internet where speech is easy to track is they dive deep into the depths of encryption where reasonable people can't disarm faulty logic.

"Social media will always, by its very nature, allow people who are like-minded to congregate and discuss," Soave said. "And that has negative consequences sometimes because, in an era before social media, someone with fringe, crazy, or even dangerous news might go their whole life living in their parents' basement thinking they are alone in their crazy views, and that's that."

The First Amendment protects you from the government censoring your speech—not private entities. Social media allows people to discuss ideas.

"Now, they might easily be able to find a couple more people who agree with them. And that can be bad. That is bad," Soave said. "That's the downside of social media, but we always have to stack that against the good things, like people with perfectly benign or even socially-beneficial views are also able to congregate and share them and produce research and new ways of thinking and improve society dramatically."

Is it ethical to ban someone from a platform? What if there are ulterior punishments, like being cut off from the best job-searching methods, cutting off internet access, or ad space for a business? In China, a low social credit score can ban someone from using public transportation, getting a low-interest loan, and a wide swath of other opportunities.

In Julius Caesar's time and before, some governments ordered people into exile, or the person could choose exile over the death penalty. The penalty, basically, equated to a death sentence unless the person could survive and be accepted elsewhere, the *Encyclopedia Britannica* says. But if you're banned from platforms today, you can keep on living in real life.

One solution pitched to "solve" the problem of people being mean to each other online is forced registration of your personal data like phone numbers connected to your state ID and address. This is a terrible idea that would hurt the most vulnerable people the most who chameleon around the internet. Can you imagine being banned from the entire internet? I pay every one of my bills via the internet. It wouldn't be livable.

You might think we're far from a version of China's "social credit system" that uses mass government and private surveillance to score residents' actions and limit free action accordingly, including buying property, acquiring loans, and even buying a plane ticket. But our tech companies are gaining more power over our lives than ever via terms and conditions agreements the majority of us didn't even read.

When Twitter, without a stated reason, restricted me from tweeting or direct messaging my stories, I was pissed. Days later, they reinstated my account posting capabilities without apology or explanation.

We should be wary of companies that hold this much power over us. Private companies are turning activist. Libertarian writer Kristin Tate explains in *The Hill* that individual companies, including PayPal, Facebook, and Microsoft are encouraging users to snitch on each other about potentially extremist content, upon which it would be banned (Tate 2021). PayPal is partnering with the left-wing Southern Poverty Law Center to "investigate" the role of "white supremacists" and propagators of "anti-government" rhetoric (Irrera 2021).

What if companies can slash our phones, internet, and freeze our bank accounts? No one but you should have the power to delete your books, movies, and music remotely.

This would lead to a terrible future. We shouldn't become a nation of snitches.

Tate writes, "At what point does free speech—be it against biological males playing in girls' sports, questioning vaccine side effects, or advocating for gun rights—make someone a target in this new system? When does your debit card get canceled over old tweets, your home loan denied for homeschooling your kids, or your eBay account invalidated because a friend flagged you for posting a Gadsden flag?" (Tate 2021).

Who decides where to draw the line? Should someone be censored or silenced for being quirky? Should I be banned or my social credit score lowered because I, a twenty-six-year-old, have both a Nerf gun and a Little Tikes basketball hoop in my apartment?

The beauty of free speech in an open forum is that the best ideas win.

When those "crazy" ideas or actors such as Alex Jones, Milo Yiannopoulos, or Bret Weinstein are pushed from the public forum into dark corners of the internet where reason and logic are absent, that's when far-right or extremist ideas spread without logical pushback. In other words, if people are planning evil things, we'd prefer them to do that on the internet where law enforcement can foil it instead of totally offline.

A study published January 2021 in *Criminology and Public Policy* found, "Despite the technical affordances that the Internet can offer, it may act as an impediment to success" to terrorists who engage in online activity compared to those who don't. Author Joe Whittaker writes: "[W]hen policy responses do focus on online interventions, it is vital to understand the unintended consequences. This is particularly the case for content removal, which may inadvertently be aiding terrorists and hampering law enforcement investigations."

When Twitter banned former President Donald Trump for allegedly inciting violence during the "storming" of the United States Capitol on January 6, it opened Pandora's Box.

Where's the line for banning someone? Should accused murderers have access to social media? What about the

Chinese Communist Party, or the Chinese Embassy in the US account, which on January 7, 2021, in a now-deleted tweet, said, "Study shows that in the process of eradicating extremism, the minds of Uyghur women in Xinjiang were emancipated, and gender equality and reproductive health were promoted, making them no longer baby-making machines. They are more confident and independent" (Davidson 2021). That's a good-sounding way to explain they forcibly sterilized women they believe are lesser beings.

That week, Twitter removed the tweet, but the looming problem remains. How will social media companies determine which domestic and foreign leaders are worthy to have an online presence? Will they block Elon Musk for his late-night, hilarious tweetstorms?

Should United States officials' social media accounts be removed for aiding and abetting government coups in other countries for "inciting violence," such as Iran's 1953 coup? What about the CIA's "MK Ultra" program, in which they, without consent, drugged hundreds of people with LSD, some of which resulted in death? What about for the US's August 29, 2021 drone strike in Afghanistan that killed nine innocent family members, seven of whom were children? (Seligman 2021).

Twitter doesn't care if you use its platform to incite violence. They care if that news hurts the platform's brand and bottom line.

But Soave ended on a positive note.

"At the end of the day, I think you have to have a little bit more faith there's more of those people, and there's more benefit to this kind of arrangement because the media only sees the negative in everything."

Even if the Big Tech giants kick you off their platform, it's not the end of the world. You might even like it. You can use search engines other than Google, such as Duckduckgo or join alternate media platforms like GETTR or Reddit. Here are some alternatives. Ditching online life may be hard, but it can also help you home in on what matters, instead of what's all the rage on the bird site.

MEWE

Ello: Pinterest/Instagram-like platform

Bitchu: YouTube alternative, although you can use YouTube without an account, which is much better. The pros and the cons are the same: there are no rules.

Minds: an anti-Facebook social platform

Myspace

Twetch

Discord

Reddit

Signal

You might even like it better on a smaller, more personalized scale, or even realize you've been dedicating too much time to life on social media instead of actually enjoying life. Focusing on long-term projects—children, building companies, a significant other, community volunteering—all bring more fulfillment, and constant distractions hurt deep work, as Cal Newport explains in *Deep Work*.

Every day we wake, we should prioritize living in the real world and enjoying whatever makes us happy to be alive.

PART 2

Part two turns to the future and is much shorter than the first section. We'll start by discussing a popular Netflix documentary that attempts to scare you rather than inform you, and why you shouldn't panic. We'll discuss how we control our own lives, and if we choose, can leave any social app we want.

The next chapters discuss how law enforcement harnesses technology in the digital world and explains why we should care about mass surveillance. The third chapter in this section zooms into China's current world, where people are tracked constantly by their faces, minorities are rounded up like cattle and thrown into detention camps, and more. This is the future we must fight against.

PART 2

CHAPTER 11

THE SOCIAL DILEMMA

———

My friends told me to watch *The Social Dilemma* on Netflix. While I didn't agree with the entire film, I'm glad the producers sparked a conversation about a topic that plagues so many of us. The film argues that social media companies abuse their power to somehow control our lives, who we like, and what we buy, and our political stance.

The film portrays social media giants manually pitching news feed content at people, sending videos on topics that are more likely to captivate the person or an update on an ex's new relationship or force them to one-click buy something. Or a meme leads you down a rabbit hole into an extremist group like the Proud Boys or Antifa that gets you arrested. But there's no reason to panic. One reason *The Social Dilemma* received rave reviews is because of slick assumptions including that social media's influence on us somehow overpowers our own volition.

There is nothing social media companies can to do stop people being mean to each other on social media. Kids and adults have been mean to one another since the dawn of time, but the platform of social media allows for bullying outside of school grounds and hours and augments already-existing cliques and shaming loners.

Moreover, who would fix it? The majority of Congress is so old they have no concept of how the internet works. In October 2021 when seventy-five-year-old Connecticut US Senator Richard Blumenthal pressed Facebook about child exploitation and associated mental health problems with the platform, he went all in.

"Will you commit to ending finsta?" he asked, not knowing the term is slang for a fake Instagram account used secretly usually to, ironically, show a more raw version of you (Wise 2021).

In Blumenthal's defense, he seemed to know what he was talking about earlier in the hearing, and he was attempting to drill down on stopping people who use anonymous accounts for evil. But it still shows the complexity of Congress revising Section 230.

WHAT GOT RIGHT

Social media is designed to be addictive, like a casino. It does exert an undue amount of influence on us. We should limit the time we spend online if we believe it's affecting us or our kids negatively. The social media industry is also designed as a "behavioralist casino" Max Read writes (Read 2020). Natasha Dow Schüll's book *Addiction by Design* calls slots the new "crack cocaine" of high-tech machine gambling where the line between human and machine, compulsion and control, risk and reward is blurred. Schüll explains how electronic gambling enters people into a trance-like "machine zone," where problems seem to dissipate, despite looming right outside the casino (ibid.).

It's nearly impossible to tell the amount of time that's passed while you're sitting in a casino. The lights are always bright, and the ceiling is colored like a blue sky. There are no windows or clocks, so you can't tell what time it is. What more could you want? All your vices are in one room: You can drink alcohol, smoke cigarettes while gambling, and even hit up sex workers afterward.

However, social media is designed to be extremely addictive to maximize screen time. Facebook didn't use to have a "feed"—you had to visit each profile. Now, the endless news feed is on the main page. Social media apps used to make you click "see more" once you got to the bottom of the page, but now, there's an infinity scroll. They removed many barriers that might lead you to log off. Their design includes seducing you to allow notifications, such as the "like" button, allowing friends to tag each other to generate more interaction (which is why they briefly allowed facial recognition to auto-tag people), a push alert a friend is going live, people's birthdays, memories of that day in previous years, activity in groups you're in and a buzz every single time someone likes or comments on a post that you did, or even that dating swipes are more likely during a certain time period.

DEPRESSION

Some studies even allege a direct correlation between social media use and depression at an alarming rate. Between 2011 and 2013, the number of teenage girls admitted to the hospital for self-harm annually out of 100,000 in the United States began steadily climbing, seemingly from nowhere, New York University Professor Jonathan Haidt explains. Haidt tweeted on January 9, 2019, that teenage nonfatal self-harm hospital visits surged 62 percent for older teen girls, and 189 percent for pre-teen girls, he says, as well as suicides.

Social media isn't the sole cause for the increase, but it appears to be a significant one of which the platform is aware, *The Wall Street Journal* reported on September 14, 2021.

"We make body image issues worse for one in three teen girls," *The Wall Street Journal* reported one 2019 Facebook slide said, summarizing research about teen girls who experience the issues. "Teens blame Instagram for increases in the rate of anxiety and depression," said another slide. "This reaction was unprompted and consistent across all groups" (ibid.).

Social media can either make you much happier through social validation or leave you digitally curb-stomped for a bad Twitter take. Especially during the early months of the COVID-19 pandemic when protecting the vulnerable meant reducing in-person interaction, I believe social media helped the mental health of young people who couldn't interact in schools, sports, or other vectors.

Journalist and personality Siraj Hashmi has over 100,000 Twitter followers who attack and insult him as well as his enemies. Nearly every week, Hashmi releases "the list" of people whose phones should be taken away, and often those people clash with followers in hilarious exchanges.

Facebook's News Feed algorithm is a secret determined from your user history that determines "personal relevancy" as it "scans and collects everything posted in the past week by each of your friends, everyone you follow, each group you belong to, and every Facebook page you like, writes Will Oremus in 2016. "The post you see at the top of your feed, then, has been chosen over thousands of others as the ones most likely to make you laugh, cry, smile, like, share, or comment."

The Power of the Like in Adolescence: Effects of Peer Influence on Neural and Behavioral Responses to Social Media, published in the National Library of Medicine, explains how posts with many likes encourage us to like it as well, and the opposite for posts with little interaction.

"Adolescents underwent fMRI while viewing photos ostensibly submitted to Instagram. They were more likely to *like* photos depicted with many likes than photos with few likes; this finding showed the influence of virtual peer endorsement and held for both neutral photos and photos of risky behaviors (e.g., drinking, smoking). Viewing photos with many (compared with few) likes was associated with greater activity in neural regions implicated in reward processing, social cognition, imitation, and attention" (ibid.).

The Social Dilemma argues social media can dominate your life: who you vote for, what products you buy, and who you date, and build division between users. Facebook knew its algorithms were divisive, *The Wall Street Journal* reported on May 26, 2020, so *The Social Dilemma* wasn't necessarily wrong.

"Our algorithms exploit the human brain's attraction to divisiveness," read a slide from a 2018 presentation. "If left unchecked," it warned, Facebook would feed users "more and more divisive content in an effort to gain user attention and increase time on the platform."

Siva Vaidhyanathan, the director of the Center for Media and Citizenship, explains in his book *Anti-Social Media*, that "Facebook engages us like a bag of chips. It offers frequent, low-level pleasures. It rarely engages our critical faculties with the sort of depth that demands conscious articulation of the experience. We might turn to Facebook in a moment of boredom and look up an hour later, wondering where that hour went and why we spent it on an experience so unremarkable yet not unpleasant" (p.35).

But in reality, you choose all of these things. Algorithms are optimized to some definition of success, mathematician Cathy O'Neil explains (O'Neil 2017). So, what are the metrics of success? Usually, an interaction is either negative or positive. One way to spike interaction rates is to create emotionally charged content, whether that's puppies playing or what appears to be people dropping off ballots in the dead of night during a presidential election.

WHAT THEY GOT WRONG

The scare tactics of *The Social Dilemma* ignore how the good of social media outweighs the negative and acts as a godsend to those in need.

After the May 2020 murder of George Floyd in police custody, rioters caused roughly $500 million of damage in the Twin

Cities. For KB Balla, that meant he had to work overtime as a firefighter for the city, saving other people's lives and property instead of defending his brand-new Scores Sports Bar. For context, in six days of riots, the St. Paul fire department responded to more than 1,150 calls (McClallen 2020). Although it was a Black-owned business, rioters torched it and the invested life savings of him, his wife, and his four young children. It wasn't insured. But the story went viral on social media, and a GoFundMe garnered over one million dollars to rebuild—one of the unlimited stories of how people use social media to help vulnerable people.

The Social Dilemma ignored the element of human choice, which drives the power of social media and advertising. Systems are bound by their users' opinions and judgments, as social networks' value is derived from how many others use the platform. Users choose to create profiles on social media accounts and choose whether to ignore an advertisement or not. Advertisements don't force people to switch from drinking White Claws to Trulys or to spend additional money, just how a smattering of movie previews in a theatre doesn't force users to binge watch fourteen movies coming out in the future.

We should minimize the exogenous negative influences that we can control that harm young, impressionable children. Another reason is loneliness, even more exacerbated by the COVID-19 pandemic that fractured friendships, in-person schools, extracurricular activities, and more which are a vital part of kids' lives. We should have the personal responsibility and individual freedom to delete apps that make life hell like Instagram or Twitter and make the best decisions for our mental and physical health by locking our phones outside our bedrooms so we can finally sleep well.

The Social Dilemma scolded social media's design to be addictive but stayed silent about Netflix's auto-play function for its 2.2 million minutes of content that, by one estimate, would take roughly four years straight to watch. If social media determines your decisions, under this logic, so does the coding of Netflix that "forced" me to binge-watch *Ozarks*. There's a blurred line between improving user experience and what some say is designing an addictive app. Infinite scroll on social media is much like a good news story lede: It pulls the consumer in—much like the beginning of movies, books, and first dates. Like writing a good lede to a story, improving social media means that it's easier to use, either way, you can still log off the app or cancel a subscription if it's a time waster.

But one thing is clear: algorithms aren't evil. Facebook and Twitter have to organize what users see, and it's in their best interest to encourage interaction and share popular content as social media evolves to pay content producers. Social media companies aren't evil, despite what *The Social Dilemma* claims. I know and have spoken to many Facebook employees who honestly believe they are changing the world, and I believe them. Moreover, I understand the outrage that Facebook knew its products might be harmful to the mental health of kids, but that meant Facebook was actively studying the problem. The company could have buried the research and covered its ass, but it didn't.

Mark Zuckerberg explains in an October 5, 2021 Facebook post.

"Many of the claims don't make any sense," he wrote. "If we wanted to ignore research, why would we create an industry-leading research program to understand these important issues in the first place? If we didn't care about fighting harmful content, then why would we employ so many more people dedicated to this than any other company in our space—even ones larger than us? If we wanted to hide our results, why would we have established an industry-leading standard for transparency and reporting on what we're doing? And if social media were as responsible for polarizing society as some people claim, then why are we seeing polarization increase in the US while it stays flat or declines in many countries with just as heavy use of social media around the world?"(ibid..).

In *The Social Dilemma*, former Google employee Tristan Harris claims that social media is a form of manipulation and says that no one got upset when people started using new tools such as bicycles. That's hilarious because that's exactly what people did.

"A bicycle is dangerous," reported the *New York Times* in 1880, "not when it is in motion, but when it is at rest. It is then that it throws its rider and tramples on him with a viciousness that the depraved horse would be ashamed to admit."

Whether it's the widespread adoption of social media, cars, or legal marijuana, there will always be fearmongers. We should weigh the pros and cons and self-regulate our actions to maximize the good while minimizing the bad. After *The Wall Street Journal*'s investigation into Facebook, the media began sensationalizing Facebook and Instagram, claiming they are "destroying democracy" and are similar to "Big

Tobacco" (Estes 2021). Rest assured, these are stupid comparisons. Cigarettes kill roughly 500,000 annually in the United States; while social media may waste tons of people's time, it's influenced the death of very few if any (CDC 2021). Don't panic and turn off sensationalist news.

The Social Dilemma dunked on social media and tech companies in a year where they were more vital than ever—working remotely through Slack, holding Zoom work meetings, and Facetiming grandparents for Christmas. Humans are social animals and require more human interaction than just tapping a screen. Social media has helped organize never-before-seen worldwide protests over the murder of George Floyd in police custody, protests over local COVID-19 restrictions, and facilitated groups in which to live stream weddings and hold spirited arguments.

And while we should be watchdogs for negative externalities of social media use, we can't ignore the incalculable benefits. It's easy to make boogeymen out of billionaire tech companies, but it's a copout to avoid creating a real argument. If we truly believe a company is evil because of how big it is, like Amazon or Facebook, then we should stop using its services.

In his October 7, 2021 newsletter Pirate Wires, venture capitalist Mike Solana explains that self-comparison to our peers is an ancient practice we continue through Instagram, *Teen Vogue*, Hollywood, and all across the internet. He argues that "isolation, alienation, [and] a struggle with identity" are problems as old as mankind that everyone faces (ibid.). He drilled down to what he sees as the root problem.

"But the difference between what Facebook does and what people do on Facebook is really the heart of this entire discussion, and the conflation of the two is why conversation on this topic has been so difficult," Solana wrote. "The thing is, we're not really asking for Facebook to control itself, we're asking Facebook to control other people" (ibid.).

The Social Dilemma blamed Big Tech for pressuring people into making certain decisions—such as attending political rallies or anger watching an ex-lover start another relationship but completely misses the point that all humans have free action to leave the platform, delete the app, or put down their phone—no matter how difficult. The film reminds me of the 1980s anti-drug commercial also intended to scare rather than inform. "This is your brain on drugs," he says as the actor cracked an egg into a pan, leaving watchers with more questions than answers.

Despite these downsides, social media offers a good number of benefits to the user such as access to their network, Facebook Groups, Marketplace, free email, and Google Docs.

Targeted ads help you. If you don't want them, use an ad blocker, then turn them off and take precautions, but you're going to be hit with ads for everyone from babies to senior citizens. Advertisers aren't evil. Products are useless if their targeted consumers don't know they exist. Moreover, the majority of the ads people are bombarded with aren't clicked on—they're skipped as soon as possible. Advertising provides a means to provide cost-free services like radio, social media, and video-streaming services that otherwise wouldn't exist in that format. Social media isn't evil—it's a neutral tool that can be used to meet a girl and fall in love or stalk them mercilessly.

We must treat social media like any other addictive substance—nicotine, alcohol, and gambling, and either constrain use or ditch it altogether. But in 2021, lacking a presence on social media could mean you don't get a job you're applying for—employers could assume you had something to hide, or currently are hiding something. Thankfully, most phones offer apps that can track screen time, cutting it off after a certain time. You can find a healthy balance of both. It just takes time and intention.

CHAPTER 12

NEW DATA POLICE

———

On May 31, 2020, a man named Michael Williams dropped off Safarain Herring, a twenty-five-year-old who was shot in the head, at a Chicago hospital. Herring died two days later (Feathers 2021).

Police pursued Williams as a prime suspect, saying video surveillance footage showed his car at the crime scene (ibid.). ShotSpotter technology uses hidden microphones citywide to detect the noise and location of gunshots and immediately alert the city. The technology is meant to distinguish between fireworks, gunshots, and vehicle exhaust combustion. On May 31, ShotSpotter technology detected a sound at 5700 South Lake Shore Drive that algorithms initially classified as a firework (ibid.). But post-alert, an analyst overrode the algorithm to be a gunshot (ibid.). Months later, another analyst changed the alert's coordinates to near Williams' car's location (ibid.). Converting police evidence to technology with no paper trail or chain of custody is a dangerous precedent that will be abused as the government adopts more tech. Often, we're convinced something is in our best interest only to have it turned against us, which in this case could lead to a years-long sentence for a crime we didn't commit.

In fewer than 120 years, we've gone from the Ford Model T to the Tesla Model S Plaid that can travel zero to sixty miles per hour in two seconds and drive autonomously, Tesla says. Such a dramatic shift of technological advances also changed policing at a rapid pace via facial recognition, predictive policing, and ShotSpotter.

Technology has transformed policing, security, and safety as we know it. We can sleep soundly and rely on home security systems to catch your son sneaking out at 2:15 a.m. instead of waiting up to bust him. Cameras can provide an independent third-party account of what happened instead of leaving it to a he-said-she-said deal. And that account is credible enough to be evidence to police or insurance agencies.

Connecting each home security system like an Amazon Ring, or just connecting neighborhoods together, can give users a network effect and track neighborhood crime patterns, Amazon support says. Using the live stream cameras collectively, they might show which way someone was running.

But why should we care about police and private surveillance? Despite widespread surveillance, you only notice cameras, license plate readers, or targeted ads if you look for them. In other words, it's easy not to care, especially when there's a global pandemic, power-hungry governments, and 6.2% inflation to consider. As the years pass, more people couldn't care less because young millennials grew up in the online world and consider themselves normal and boring. While we might not care now, we likely will in the future when the wrong people get access to our information.

Once the government or another entity has your data (pictures, videos, journals), they have it forever—even if it's a video or incident from one of the worst days of our life. Possibly, that content could overturn a campaign for public office, or spark a divorce. And our data is intertwined with that of our friends and family, our collective privacy. Cambridge Analytica gathered data from 270,000 Facebook users before the 2016 presidential election (Veliz 2019). Instead of only getting data from the users they targeted, they initially obtained the personal information of eighty-seven million people, which is the size of the United Kingdom plus twenty million people—the original users' friends who didn't directly consent (ibid.) (Worldometer UK population 2021).

Similarly, all our lives are intertwined—where we shop, eat, the shows and news we watch, and the neighborhoods we live in. A Detroit teenager's wrongful arrest because of facial recognition could mean you don't meet your significant other, or derail that person's career. This is why the justice system would rather let a killer walk free than lock up an innocent man. Similarly, we should structure data protections by prioritizing the least harm.

Williams' story and many like it are why we should care about privacy and properly reined police technology so that innocent people don't face prison because of a computer's mistake.

Once something goes online, it's there forever. We may think our tweets, likes, and statuses on social media are for our own purpose, but in reality, they're being scraped for your information. Thousands of data points—your age, interests, the name of your first dog, the street you grew up on, your mother's maiden name—are pulled and processed per day from Facebook, Twitter, Instagram, and other platforms (Ferguson 2017, 2)

Law enforcement is much different now than it was twenty years ago. Now, they are on Twitter and Facebook, and some of their accounts are hilarious.

An algorithm determined by Miles Wernick of the Illinois Institute of Technology uses variables to grant individuals' risk scores of who will likely be involved in a crime (Kaplan 2017). Nearly 4,000 Chicagoans have a risk profile score determined by a partially secret algorithm, but here's what we know (ibid.). Seven risk factors determine your score:

- Age at most recent arrest (the younger, the higher the score)

- If you have been a shooting victim

- If you have been an assault victim

- Violent crime arrests

- Unlawful use of weapon arrests

- Narcotics arrests

- Trend in criminal activity (either increasing or decreasing) (ibid.).

So, what this means is that if you just happen to be in the background of a suspect's photographs, you can end up in that database, guilty by association just for being in the wrong place at the wrong time.

Police use "predictive policing" to mark "hot" areas for each hour of the day, American University College of Law Professor of Law Andrew Guthrie Ferguson explains in *The Rise of Big Data Policing* (Ferguson 2017).

Some progress was made with targeted help. From 2011 to 2014, New Orleans saw a 21.9 percent reduction in homicides and a 55 percent drop in group or gang-related murders (ibid.). Months later, on Memorial Day, 78 percent of the 64 people shot were on the list (ibid.). Police will more heavily rely on big data and predictive policing, including facial recognition drones and police robot dogs (Shackford 2019). At least 18,000 police departments nationwide use facial recognition software (Burke 2021).

In Jackson, Mississippi, police are conducting a pilot program to live stream security cameras, including Ring, then compile them in a Real-Time Crime Center to cut down on crime (Guariglia 2021). A company called Fusus sells the software and contracts with police departments in Minnesota, Georgia, California, and Illinois (Holmes 2020). It's hard to argue against this sort of technology if it could provide clear, compelling evidence of a crime. Police can use tech to better identify and connect criminals, but they must use tech carefully to prevent jailing innocent people and giving weapons to police robot dogs. A security camera can give police a description of a homicide suspect when they might otherwise have no leads, but the re-recorded, grainy film also might point police in the wrong direction if the facial recognition fails.

Tech is a neutral tool. In her 2008 dissent in *Herring v. United States*, the late Supreme Court Justice Ruth Bader Ginsburg raised a warning flag early on of intertwined, often clumsily kept government databases that can result in government tyranny.

"Inaccuracies in expansive, interconnected collections of electronic information raise grave concerns for individual liberty," she wrote. "The offense to the dignity of the citizen who is arrested, handcuffed, and searched on a public street simply because some bureaucrat has failed to maintain an accurate computer data base is evocative of the use of general warrants that so outraged the authors of the Bill of Rights" (ibid.). Ginsburg knew the law should be based on Blackstone's ratio, that "It is better that ten guilty persons escape than that one innocent suffer."

A citizen who is wrongfully arrested in public, in front of family and strangers, will never forget. On January 9, 2020, the Detroit Police Department (DPD) wrongly arrested Robert Williams in front of his wife and daughters, ages two and five, for allegedly swiping five watches costing $3,800 from a Shinola retail store. When William's wife asked where they were taking him, an officer responded, "Google it" (Allyn 2020).

Police detained Williams, a Black man, for nearly thirty hours against his will before admitting "the computer must have gotten it wrong" (ibid..). Actually, the police got it wrong. DPD says it's enacted new rules (McClallen 2020). Now only photos can be used for facial recognition, only used in violent crimes (ibid..). But there's not enough retribution available for a wrongful arrest based on no evidence.

However, facial recognition can help police stop bad guys by analyzing digital books of as many as 400,000 mugshots (ibid..). After a potential match occurs, the detectives must investigate further. Deputy Chief David LeValley said the claim that the technology is only 4 percent accurate is misleading because that's about the accuracy rate if police chose the first image produced (ibid..). The software ranks roughly the top fifty photos (ibid..).

"The efficiency that we gain from using facial recognition is tremendous," Detroit Deputy Chief Marlon Wilson told the City Council in September 2020. "A lot of these cases would just be a 'who-done-it.'" (ibid..).

In September of 2020, Detroit Police Capt. Aric Tosqui said the technology was used 106 times that year, resulting in sixty-four matches, and assisting in twelve arrests (ibid.). Even if the video doesn't expose a suspect, it may show the car or description of the criminal.

LEGAL LOOPHOLES?

The government and law enforcement can also use this data to skirt the Fourth Amendment via loopholes by searching our digital property. On February 22, 2021, *The Wall Street Journal* reported the Defense Intelligence Agency said it has access to "commercially available consumer apps" from the US and abroad—and there's a huge market for such data pulled from data for advertising and other commercial purposes. It said it had queried its database to look at the location information of US-based smartphones five times in the last two and a half years as part of authorized investigations (ibid.).

On January 2, 2021, *The Wall Street Journal* revealed that US government agencies buy data from commercial brokers without a warrant, raising questions about whether those agencies were adequately safeguarding Americans' privacy and civil liberties (Tau 2021).

The Internal Revenue Service also purchased access to cellphone data as part of its law enforcement mission (Tau 2020). All claim because the data is purchased on the open market, no court order is required.

"The abuses here take your breath away, and it really is a dodge on all the legal protections Americans have," Wyden said about US efforts to collect data (Tau 2021). "I'm particularly troubled by the intelligence community's purchases of Americans' private data. It's almost like getting around the whole question of people's privacy rights. And so transparency is crucial," Wyden said (ibid.).

The data drawn from cellphones can be used to create maps of suspects' real-world social networks—even if they use disposable "burner" phones or use anonymizing technologies. That technology is of interest to both intelligence agencies and law enforcement (ibid.). The IRS says the tech would be useful for "tracking targets who keep multiple phones, or who drop their phones frequently since you can search for phones that are frequently [in] the same location as another phone" (ibid.).

Should government spend taxpayer money on data to circumvent the Fourth Amendment? Does the IRS need to know my exact location so it can break my legs if I don't pay? We need to halt the enormous privacy violations committed by the US Government. Why can the government buy my data when they would otherwise need to have probable cause and a warrant? Would the Founding Fathers be chill with this?

Matthew Guariglia, a policy analyst at the Electronic Frontier Foundation, said these policing advances have real harm. He argues that when police technology innovates, police rely more and more on technology to tell whom to arrest rather than detective work. Guariglia argued that law enforcement relies too heavily on technology instead of the long hours of detective work.

For example, grainy security footage input into facial recognition software can lead to wrongful arrests. Software is only as good as its inputs. Most surveillance cameras are mounted at an angle different from photos taken for a driver's license, mugshot, or Facebook, and if compiled with poor lighting and low-quality image resolution, it can produce false hits, according to a December 2012 study. For Williams, that meant the government threw him in a cage for nearly thirty hours before law enforcement realized its mistake. Facial recognition is less accurate for females, Blacks, and subjects eighteen to thirty years old, compared to other races and ages of people (ibid.). Critics say those statistics pose problems, especially in Detroit since Motor City's population is approximately 80 percent Black. Officers argue they only use facial recognition to speed up investigations—and then put in the real investigative work.

Guariglia says the use of facial recognition should be banned, as should predictive policing because surveillance is disproportionately located in large cities where a diverse type of people live.

"Predictive policing doesn't predict crime," he said. "What it does is criminalize a person's proximity to crime. If you have a cousin who's been to jail, or if you live in a neighborhood where there are a lot of muggings, if you've been the victim of crime in the past, all of these are likely to land you on a list of potential criminals and make you eligible for constant harassment and surveillance."

He says trust between the community and police is key to stopping crime.

"When it comes to crime, especially, collaboration and trust between government and the people in the community is one of the best deterrents. Because when you think of what surveillance does, it takes the place of an uncooperative public."

"I believe the question of whether you can have security or privacy is a false dichotomy."

Accuracy concerns also exist with consumer data published for fun but repurposed for criminal investigations. When you upload pictures to the internet, our phone's embedded our identity and "geotag" location. Retailers also use this function, as does Snapchat and, by proxy, the federal government (Ferguson 2017, 96).

As police adopt more technology, we must hold them accountable to Constitutional protections and ensure we don't arrest innocent people because of technological difficulties.

Anti-police sentiment has been accumulating for years, thanks to a police state augmented by qualified immunity and police unions that prohibit the firing of bad cops. However, police play a vital part in society. Even those critical of police and advocate for reform likely agree that responding to a hostage situation, a domestic dispute, or many other emergency calls can be a nightmare. Still, many police show up to work daily even though they could be killed any day.

That's why Americans granted law enforcement a monopoly on the use of force and to some extent, surveillance to remove bad actors so they won't hurt others. In return, we check their power with rights, judges, and rulebooks. If there's credible evidence someone is breaking the social code, police can use their powers. But only then. And otherwise, we should be left alone. There's a delicate social contract between citizens and police, and that fiber has been fraying for the last several decades. Residents surrender some liberty to submit to the authority of police if they have credible evidence of you breaking a law, like speeding. The majority of police officers cause few citizen complaints and lawsuits, according to a 2017 Dolan Consulting Group research brief that "about 5 percent of the officers on these agencies were responsible for all of the sustained citizen complaints" (Johnson 2017).

We should be careful with leaps in police tech advancement and verify data policing. People are more complicated than risk scores, but I think the information, if used carefully, could save lives.

The Bill of Rights, along with property rights, fundamentally contributes to a free society. If police or strangers could barge into your home at any time, loot your safe, and steal your wife, we would act differently. We would spend the majority of our time defending what we already have instead of creating more value and augmenting the size of the economic pie. In that way, police jumpstart economic growth.

CHAPTER 13

THE FUTURE OF FACIAL RECOGNITION: CHINA

———

When a Shenfenbao salesman named Lin Jiahong searched a common name of real-time records of about 1,200 hotels in the 650-square mile city of Xiamen, China, Jiahong found three people instantly—and their hotels, room numbers, time of check-in, registered address, ethnicity, and age (Paul and Krolik 2019).

Xiamen, China is roughly the same population as Los Angeles with 3.79 million people, a travel guide says. This is just one example of how powerful current tech is. Tech is a tool that can be used for good or evil. In the last 250 years, tech, generally, has helped the world by leaps and bounds like the Industrial Revolution and Digital Age. But in the next fifty years, tech could twist a dream into a nightmare. We're surrendering more information than ever before through social media, online profiles, and living online. But we should think about why companies and government want our data and the worst possible outcomes. Constant surveillance can leave few secrets even in a city as large as Los Angeles—the second most populated city in the US. A glance into China shows why you shouldn't trust the government with private data, advanced surveillance, or control of the internet. Advanced technology allows the Chinese government to surveil ethnicities they don't like, including roughly eleven million Uyghurs—a predominantly Muslim ethnic minority who live in the Xinjiang region (Paul and Krolik 2019).

The Chinese Communist government views the Uyghurs as a threat because some have sought greater autonomy (Shesgreen 2021). Facial recognition plus other tech that controls our lives, such as our payment systems, computers, fingerprints, and DNA can be weaponized. China has the "largest video surveillance network in the world and plans to expand it to more than 600 million cameras over the next two years," a Vice Documentary says. This surveillance is used to control the Uyghur population, leading to the Chinese government's ability to sterilize much of their population. Historian James Milward says every 100 feet, Uyghurs must pass police checkpoints in which they must scan ID, irises, and cell phones (Milward 2018). Experts with the Australian Strategic Policy Institute have identified at least 380 detention facilities in Xinjiang that have been newly built or expanded since 2017. Some estimates put the number of detention facilities as high as 1,400 (ibid.).

The revelations underscore how Xinjiang is an early exploration into the future of all-encompassing technology, like smartphones, widespread cheap digital camera systems, and mass online storage of data that combine to monitor and repress large groups of people when civil liberties concerns are pushed aside. Their government now has technology that can identify everyone in a crowd of up to thirty people "within a second," Hanwang Vice President Huang Lei told Reuters.

It's hard to understand how or why a government would abuse its power to oppress minorities and vulnerable people who have few methods to fight back, but it's up to us to check our government from such things. The government shouldn't determine social credit scores that allow your freedom and ability to travel and get loans. The government should provide basic services instead of controlling people and taking over industries about which it knows little. For example in 2019, the Canadian government lost over thirty million in US dollars selling marijuana (Shackford 2019).

China's creepy surveillance state is an augmented problem of the government's centralized control. The Chinese government feels the need to control the economy, which companies boom and bust, and even what they search on the internet. Winnie the Pooh didn't even make the cut because some think he resembles Chinese President Xi Jinping (Haas 2018). Neither did the Chinese government's 1989 Tiananmen Square massacre. China knew people are hard to control, but it did the next best thing: Install the most cameras per capita in the world so they can bust people breaking the law because it doesn't trust its own residents. Under constant surveillance, people act differently and self-censor.

"The fact that you *won't* do things, that you will self-censor, are the worst effects of pervasive surveillance," Bruce Schneier, a former fellow at the Berkman and in the cybersecurity program of the Kennedy School's Belfer Center for Government and

International Affairs told Harvard's magazine. "Governments, of course, know this. China bases its surveillance on this fact. It *wants* people to self-censor because it knows it can't stop everybody. The idea is that if you don't know where the line is, and the penalty for crossing it is severe, you will stay far away from it."

The effectiveness of surveillance at preventing crime or terrorism can be debated, but "If your goal is to control a population," Schneier says, "mass surveillance is awesome."

We should use tech for its benefits, but tech alone shouldn't send someone to prison. Much like how powerful modern-day phones can do incredible things but we use them to stream Netflix and watch animal videos online, we have to be smart about our tech use. While technology and AI are impressive, the human brain is even more incredible.

In a world under mass surveillance, there is no such thing as anonymity or secrets. You can pay for your food with your face, which also controls how much toilet paper you get. Your face replaced your apartment key—meaning the government can track when you're home, when you leave, and who visits, and how long they stay. And they've used that information about as well as can be expected. This tech could be convenient but at the cost of our freedom and privacy. In China, most people don't use credit cards. They pay with mobile phones (even beggars), which is convenient but also means the government knows every one of your transactions—who it was with and what it was.

Having options means having a choice and freedom whether you want to charge a credit card, use Bitcoin, or cash. In

January 2021, *The Intercept* reported China holds millions of files on Uyghurs, and other minorities like Uyghurs, Kazakhs, and Kyrgyz.

"The mass surveillance in Xinjiang is a cautionary tale for all of us," Maya Wang, China senior researcher at Human Rights Watch, told *The Intercept*. "Xinjiang really shows how privacy is a gateway right, where if you have no privacy, that's where you see that you have no freedoms as a human being at all. You don't have the right to practice your religion; you don't have the right to be who you are; you don't even have the right to think your own thoughts because your thoughts are being parsed out by these incessant visits and incessantly monitored by surveillance systems, whether they're human or artificial, and evaluated constantly for your level of loyalty to the government" (ibid.).

"This group has over 200 ethnic-language people," the order stated. "Many of them are relatives of incarcerated people. Recently, many intelligence reports revealed that there is a tendency for relatives of [extremist] people to gather. This situation needs major attention. After receiving this information, please investigate immediately. Find out the background of the people who organize free travel, their motivation, and the inner details of their activities (ibid.).

Estimates suggest more than a million Uyghurs and other minorities have been detained in camps in China. A 2021 investigation published by the *BBC* contained first-hand testimony of systematic rape, sexual abuse, and torture of women detainees by police and guards in those camps. China's foreign ministry has denied the allegations, accusing the

BBC of making a "false report" and later banned the network from China (ibid.).

The Xinjiang region is a rising star in the solar power panel supply chain field fueled by Uyghur slave labor (Copley 2020). In 2019, when solar ranked as the world's top source of new power generating capacity, about one-third of the solar panel derivatize polysilicon came from Xinjiang, according to Johannes Bernreuter of Bernreuter Research. China as a whole accounts for about 80 percent of global capacity (ibid.).

GRABBY GOVERNMENT

The Intercept explained that police documents reflect an intent to hunt down suspicious behavior of any kind. But who decides what's suspicious? Is walking the dog, going to a house of worship, or returning home late at night or early morning suspicious?

The core problem of this system is that once you pay taxes and fulfill minimum requirements, the government should leave you alone. The more power you give the government, the more they pry into your personal life when government's only job is to protect property rights and provide basic services. We have to remember that the government's role is to protect property rights and provide basic services that we fund through taxes. So, we should fund public safety and police but limit it before that tech is used to pry into our lives.

"The system is set up in a way that's producing hyperpolicing," Darren Byler, an anthropologist and postdoctoral researcher at the Center for Asian Studies at the University of Colorado

Boulder, told *The Intercept*. "Where any strange or any kind of aberrant behavior is reported, and if you're a minority, you're 'ethnic,' which is how they refer to Uyghurs and Kazakhs, then you're very susceptible to this kind of stuff, and you're being policed on a micro level, both by human policing and by the application of the technology to you and your life."

Once the government takes a freedom or right away, it's hard to get it back.

The government reasons that constant surveillance can determine whether you're a "good citizen" that doesn't speed or litter or spit outside. And if you're bad enough, China will trap you and ruin your life by prohibiting you from buying flight or plane tickets, property, or getting a loan (Kobie 2019). Liu Hu, a blacklisted journalist in China told *The Globe* and *Mail* about China's social credit system ranking almost 1.4 billion people (Vanderklippe 2018). "There was no file, no police warrant, no official advance notification. They just cut me off from the things I was once entitled to," he said. "What's really scary is there's nothing you can do about it. You can report to no one. You are stuck in the middle of nowhere." (ibid.).

Sesame Credit sounds like a children's show, but it grants China's credit scores influenced by the rank of your friends, the model of the car you drive, your job, education level, and more (ibid.). Being friends with people with low credit hurts your own.

The base problem with social credit systems and algorithm rules is that they can be wrong and manipulated and very few people would know (or care). China's "Golden Shield," an online surveillance tool can suspend internet access and social media accounts if that person speaks against the government, meaning mentioning "Tibetan independence" or "Tiananmen Square incident," or Winnie the Pooh because the character has a striking resemblance to President Xi Jinping.

ADVANCED TECH AND SOCIAL CREDIT SYSTEMS

The FBI's Next General Identification system has around fifty-two million searchable faces and uses DNA, facial recognition, iris scans, and voice samples (Ingraham 2014). The INTERPOL Face Recognition System (IFRS) contains facial images from more than 160 countries out of 195—a global criminal database. The Georgetown Law Center on Privacy and Technology released a 2016 study that found law enforcement recognition networks include over 117 million American adults (Nelson 2016). According to "State of AI 2020" created by Nathan Benaich and Ian Hogarth, general partner of Air Street Capital, and angel investor Ian Hogarth, over half of the world allows facial recognition, while only three countries—Belgium, Luxembourg, and Morocco have partial bans on the technology.

Hundreds of cities in China require citizens to use cell phone software to classify each person with a color code showing their contagion risk—red, yellow, or green. The software determines which people should be quarantined or permitted to enter public places like subways" (Paul, Zhong, Krolik 2020).

In Indian Kerala, India, authorities used telephone call records, surveillance camera footage, and phone location data to track down people who may have been in contact with coronavirus patients" (Srivasrava and Nagaraj 2020). Some parts of India were stamping the hands of people arriving at airports telling them how long they had to be quarantined, Reuters reported (ibid.). The government monitored airline and train reservation data to ensure those people didn't travel (ibid.).

Fintech uses a version of this program in Kenya, Ronald J. Deibert explains in his book *Reset: Reclaiming the Internet for Civil Society* (p. 62–63). "Many Kenyans report receiving them late at night on weekends, when their defences might be down because of alcohol consumption. An app called OKcash even goes so far as to harvest users' contacts then call bosses, parents, and friends to shame defaulters into repaying" (ibid.).

The ACLU explains why that will lead to privacy concerns (Stanley 2018).

"The heart of the problem with tracking apps and the rest of our corrupted privacy regime is that it has been built around the concept of "notice and consent": As long as a company includes a description of what it is doing somewhere in an arcane, lengthy, fine-print click-through "agreement," and the consumer "agrees"—which they must do to utilize a service—then the company can argue that it has met its privacy obligations" (ibid.).

The goal is to instill fear into others and values of their citizens, but that could turn evil fast, such as some sick form of justification to eliminate or make life hell for "bad" citizens with low scores. The idea is to incentivize good citizens, but who decides what a "good citizen" is? Are they forced to be patriotic? Does that require forced kneeling for the national anthem, not burning flags, and barbecuing on Friday evening, or watching baseball? Do they have to like apple pie? Do they have to support local businesses instead of ordering products online? Do they have to follow the speed limit? Do they have to stop consuming unhealthy foods, smoking, and drinking excessively? Who made the grading rubric? Are loners bad for society and reason for suspicion? Even if we're not, people act differently when they know they're being watched.

Reason writer Jacob Sullum has pointed out, "Knowing that you are being watched by armed government agents tends to put a damper on things (Sullum 2002). You don't want to offend them or otherwise call attention to yourself." Eventually, he warns, "people may learn to be careful about the books and periodicals they read in public, avoiding titles that might alarm unseen observers. They may also put more thought into how they dress, lest they look like terrorists, gang members, druggies, or hookers" (ibid.).

Can the government pressure people into being healthy? Into using less water and electricity? It's in the government's best interest to do so—along with regular exercise, less alcohol, and regular doctor's visits. The German government mandates dog owners to walk their dogs twice per day (Connolly 2020). It'd be cheaper for the government if people ate healthier, exercised consistently, and squashed bad habits. But people choose freely how to act. Instead of "should we," we should ask, "Why would we?"

To summarize, government should leave us alone if we pay taxes. The idea that the government should monitor every

American's transactions over $600 while our government goes on an opaque trillion-dollar spending spree with our tax dollars is ludicrous. We the people fund the government, and we should hold them to account for how that money is spent.

Giving the government the power to enact social credit systems is like creating another Jurassic Park: it's only a matter of time until something goes terribly wrong. Sometimes, society is too complex for the government to legislate or attempt to centrally control. Consider crazy COVID-19 rules when the government deemed some businesses as "essential" and shuttered others. Today's technology is mind-blowing. We should ensure government uses it to help people instead of enslaving them. Technology can quickly be turned against people. As long as we pay taxes and follow the law, the government should leave us alone. Our private information is none of the government's business. We could press government to completely ban this tech, but we'd lose the advantage of it as well. We should use this technology but enact stringent safeguards held accountable by humans.

PART 3

This is the final section where we analyze how tech can cause modern-day miracles like helping the blind "see" again, provide internet to billions of people, and help people in their everyday life by reminding them to live well and attend regular doctor checkups. After several chapters diving into dark details of technological abuse, these chapters are meant to show the widespread good that tech accomplishes every day. I'll discuss how tech acts as an equalizer between the rich and poor, how we should use the COVID-19 pandemic to reset our online and real-life lives, and how we can use the internet to facilitate civil conversation with people who believe different things than we do. I also argue for tossing "legalese" in everyday contracts and terms and conditions that nobody, but lawyers can understand.

PART 3

CHAPTER 14

FOUR REASONS FOR HOPE

———

Technology is an equalizer worldwide and the driving force of human freedom, whether that means providing new, better, or cheaper services that jumpstart opportunity for outsiders, dreamers, immigrants with big ideas, and overall rabble-rousers. We've covered many ways tech can be abused, but here are four ways that tech will improve the quality of life around the world.

EQUALIZER

Just one hundred years ago, kings and peasants lived an utterly different quality of life, and in 1929, the Great Depression ravaged the economy and scarred people for life. Now, crucial metrics show the quality of life in most countries is better and better, thanks to technology and the crazy people who choose it as a career.

In 1950, 75 percent of the world lived in extreme poverty, defined as living on a daily cost of $1.90 (Roser 2016). In 2015, less than

10 percent of the world was living in extreme poverty (ibid.). Before the Industrial Revolution, your standard of living was directly related to your income. Kings used to thrive while the kingdom's residents starved. But our evolution and the Industrial Revolution changed everything. Suddenly, mass production made more and cheaper cars widely available than ever before, providing new tech to rich and poor Americans alike, Investopedia explains. It didn't just drive car prices down, but goods that were once luxuries, and across-the-board, thanks to technology (ibid.). Similar to the widespread enactment of the printing press, there was no going back.

In 2020, technology still acted as an equalizer between the rich and poor. We all use the same phones, log in to Gmail accounts, and use the same social media sites as celebrities and millionaires. In 1984, Apple's first computer cost $2,500 (Wichowski 2020, 21). I just bought a much better Macbook for just over $1,000. "If you had bought the computing power found inside an iPhone 5S in 1991, it would have cost you $3.56 million" (Rosoff 2014).

The value of my Google account is priceless. I've written over 5,000 articles, papers, and the entirety of this book in Google Docs, which my Grammarly tracker says exceeds 3.6 million words checked. My four Gmail accounts hold thousands of interviews and exciting conversations. Thousands of pictures stored in Google Drive show friends and family, some of whom are now dead. Other contents include massive data sets, Freedom of Information Act documents, and "unreleased" albums by now-deceased rapper Mac Miller.

Because of tech companies, we can pay $8.99 per month to stream content instead of paying a cable company $150 per month, and if you pay for Hulu, content is released same-day as theaters. YouTube's music algorithm knows my music preferences better than I do.

But I pay no monetary cost for many of these services. What are your online profiles worth to you? Tech prices have fallen so low that almost everybody can have phones and laptops. Many homeless people have cell phones, meaning vital tech reaches even the most impoverished. Free services let people spend more income on enjoying life, and pretty soon, the internet might reach much more of the world.

Roughly 3.7 billion people still don't have internet access worldwide, which Elon Musk is trying to change through the Starlink satellite internet (Houser 2021). SpaceX has launched about 1,100 of the planned 10,000 Starlink satellites (Houser 2020). The network is still in the beta phase, with about 10,000 users (Sheetz 2020). SpaceX's Starlink satellite internet has the potential to bridge the digital divide. Now, SpaceX has asked the FCC permission to begin selling terminals attachable to vehicles, such as trucks, airplanes, and boats (but not passenger cars—the terminals are too big, Musk tweeted on April 8, 2021. If granted permission, the Starlink satellite internet network could be mobile to anywhere drivable (Houser 2021).

TECH HELPS THE MOST VULNERABLE

No shade to Jesus Christ of Nazareth, but some tech can make the blind "see" again (Stepko 2021). The OrCam MyEye Pro is a camera that attaches to glasses that use touch, sound, feel, and hearing to describe their world (ibid.). So, if you want to know what's in front of you, you tap a button, and the camera will take a picture and then audibly describe the image via a speaker (ibid.). About twelve million people in the US have low or no vision from a range of eye diseases that steal precious moments like seeing a grandchild or watching the sunrise (ibid.). The glasses, equipped with facial recognition, can audibly identify the people it sees, even if the user has dementia and can't always remember. The device costs $4,250 (ibid.). WeWALK is an intelligent cane that detects obstacles and has a built-in GPS to connect to a phone to identify bus numbers (ibid.).

There are also new monetary lending programs including the nonprofit Kiva that service third-world countries, some of which are getting internet access and a path to a better life. Thanks to the internet and Kiva, 3.9 million people from up to seventy-seven countries have borrowed $1.6 billion to fund their business, education, or a range of other items (ibid.). Kiva's lent to 1.26 million people in the least-developed countries (ibid.). In Indonesia, that meant Padimah got her $800 loan to build a pump to get clean water for her family (ibid.). In Palestine, Ahmed got his $3,000 loan to send his son to school (ibid.). In El Salvador, Graciela Emilia got her $500 loan to pay laborers to sow staples grains (ibid.). Although the borrowers and lenders will likely never meet; technology allows us to help each other from over 6,000 miles away.

Many people feel giddy the first time someone uses the internet to send a text or another message. I remember the first time I could send text messages and even picture messages. In India and across the world in Asia, the Middle East, and Africa, more people are getting online than ever before and sending good morning texts, often filling up low-memory phones (Purnell 2018).

Remote work might inconvenience many of us, but for those with developmental disabilities, including autism, in which the person prefers to control their work environment, dodge social pressure, and make their own schedule, it can be a godsend (Samuel 2021).

TECH CAN HELP COMPANIES THRIVE

Ask any entrepreneur: Starting a business can be hard but staying in business in the long run is the greatest challenge. Companies can harness tech to analyze their business and work smarter with fewer costs now and in the future. Companies can use tech to close the gap for asymmetric information and moral hazard to fix so-called market failures—when one party to an economic transaction has more or better information than another and uses that to their advantage.

A market failure, defined by Investopedia, is "the economic situation defined by an inefficient distribution of goods and services in the free market. In market failure, the individual incentives for rational behavior do not lead to rational outcomes for the group" (ibid.). One market failure is moral hazard, when two parties involved in a transaction have differing amounts of information that affects the parties' action. One "market failure" is adverse selection, such as when you buy insurance for a rental vehicle and then take it off-roading because there's no additional cost born by you. For example, an insurance company's Bluetooth beacon in your vehicle tracking your driving, braking, and phone use can better determine your "good driver" discount instead of more broadly bundling driver's risk factors. In short, your insurance company would receive more accurate information, and you would pay the actual cost of your driving habits and record.

Currently, this so-called "discount" collects data from months to overview driving, but that could be per day or trip in the future.

For example, your vehicle could incentivize you to take a sobriety test before starting it when driving late hours or during excessive hours on the road in a row (sleep-deprived driving is worse than or equal to drunk driving).

A McKinsey report on the future of insurance concludes: "Uncertainty will be strongly reduced." This might help private companies test products by tracking selling amounts before diving into a $100,000 venture. Companies know more and more about us, and there's no clear way to separate the good that technology brings from the bad surveillance and data market. We should limit and decide where we stand on the tradeoff between privacy and letting companies use our data and what we post on the internet. Are we willing to sacrifice our Apple Watch exercise privacy to get a more significant health insurance premium for working out three times per week for thirty minutes as you agreed, are consuming your suggested actual calorie consumption, or avoiding binge drinking and inhaling nicotine?

Companies will stop asking what pain point people want fixed and watch what ails them instead—a better step for companies because people's actions better predict true behavior than what we say we will do. Data collection isn't essential for companies to survive, but it can help a lot.

The Amazon Halo measures and tracks people's emotions throughout the day. They'll likely find people who are stressed, sleep-deprived, and unfulfilled. For example, for a hundred dollars, plus a recurring fee, you can buy an Amazon Halo, which has two microphones in it and apparently can make a 3D rendering of your body, track your body fat percentage, sleep, and even emotions.

There are billions of ways tech helps us every day. We just need to draw privacy boundaries on what we want publicly known with one Google search.

Businesses harness tech to entice each customer, whether through coupons, low prices, or exclusive offers. For example, data brokers can sell our eating habits and the day and hours you typically order takeout every week. And during those hours, companies can pay for direct advertising during peak order hours. In East Lansing, Michigan, that means one of the second-tier bars can "steal" students waiting in line for hours at first-tier bars by directly advertising to Spartans via their phones via geofencing.

BETTER DECISIONS

We can use tech to nudge most people's decisions via texts or emails and then let the person decide. Behavioral economist Richard Thaler won a Nobel Prize for his Nudge Theory that could provide people with more information about options to better decisions. If we use tech right, we can harness it to live longer, fuller, and better lives.

Improve your health: Use tech to keep you accountable. Use your Snapchat story and your followers to hold you accountable to work out regularly. Track your calories. Maybe most importantly, documenting your fitness journey shows its possible and might inspire others. I believe social media as a concept is good, but we just use it for harmful purposes, like one Chicago rapper calling out another rapper on Twitter who in response murdered the person. We should treat Facebook and social media like talking to people who are rooting for you instead of attacking you.

So, on a morning you don't feel like working out, you can see your friends didn't skip leg day, so neither can you. We can reinforce each other by liking each other's LinkedIn posts or commenting on a friend's new baby pictures, job changes, or fall pictures. Even if you're physically isolated from friends or family, everyone is just a text or call away.

On social media, you're the main character in a world of billions, but your followers should support you. I sourced $2,500, half the funding for this book via Facebook alone, some from people who've never met me. We should keep our social circle small, stay close with family members who could live a world away, and maximize the utility of social media—telling people happy birthday, post jokes, photo dumps—while dodging ensuing depression or endless comparison of your life to your friends' lives and instead add reminders to read, add time limits to toxic apps, etc.

One example is automatically setting new drivers as organ donors and letting them choose if they don't want to be one.

Demand for organ transplants outstrips supply, partly because organ sales are illegal. In 2019, 19,267 donors made a record-setting 39,718 transplants possible, but nearly 109,000 Americans remain on the organ transplant waiting list (Reichel 2020). We can combine nudging more people onto the list with designing algorithms to streamline transplants to donors.

Most people don't change factory settings, whether that's a phone notification sounds or whether you automatically opt into your 401(k) or not. In the book *Nudge: Improving Decisions About Health, Wealth, and Happiness*, Richard Thaler and Cass R. Sunstein explain that "nudges" can help someone improve their life without restricting their freedom. Nudges suggest one decision for a question in which there's a more significant benefit to improve welfare but ultimately leaves the decision to the person.

In 2006, Washington lawmakers applied Thaler's research to reform America's 401(k) system by asking employers to enroll workers into the system automatically but offer the right to opt out (Thaler and Benzarti 2004). How significant is the impact of auto-enrollment? One 2015 Vanguard paper suggested that the practice more than doubled plan participation rates to more than 91 percent of workers from 42 percent (Salisbury 2017).

You might have yawned as soon as I said 401(k), but this tweak benefits millions of lives. Compound interest means early money invested can quadruple over decades and provide freedom.

Investopedia explains: "A single $10,000 investment at age twenty would grow to over $70,000 by the time the investor was sixty years old (based on a 5 percent interest rate). That same $10,000 investment made at age thirty would yield about $43,000 by age sixty and made at age forty would yield only $26,000 (Folger 2021).

The government is crazy, and we live in a clown world. As of September 2021, the federal government came close to shutting down. You shouldn't count on the government or politicians to save you from student loans, Big Tech's censorship, or basically anything else. We must seize control of our lives and handle our problems, whether that's by sacrificing lifestyle choices while paying off loans we signed or deleting your Facebook because you're tired of being censored.

Just how we budget our time, a nudge to budget our money for retirement and the rest of our lives could only help us. Americans are notorious for not saving enough for retirement and living on the financial edge of bankruptcy. The Department of Labor estimates only 40 percent of Americans have calculated how much they need to save for retirement. In 2018, almost 30 percent of private-sector workers with a 401(k) didn't participate (ibid.). Moreso, a 2013 survey found that 50 percent of all adults would have difficulty paying for a $400 emergency expense, with nearly 20 percent not being able to pay (Grover 2021).

Financial nudges could change the lives of millions of families. A 401(k) with $500,000 might seem like just money, but it's also freedom and opportunity to place a parent in a specialized care facility instead of a Medicaid nursing home. If you've saved money for decades and planned your financial future, the next time your boss denies your time-off request to travel to a family member's funeral, you can walk out the door for the last time without worrying about how you'll pay bills. If you, your significant other, or your child is struck with a life-threatening disease that requires life-altering amounts of money, travel, and medicine, you can sell your house or cash in retirement accounts. If we let tech help us, it could induce financial freedom to millions of people.

We have smart tech, but we use it for dumb purposes like watching hours of cat videos and getting lost in Reddit forums (both of which have their place). But we could use tech to create the healthiest, happiest, and most empowered versions of ourselves.

If done encrypted, our personal data could encourage us to stop doomscrolling, binge-watching Netflix, and driving drunk, and instead go for a walk or to the gym, or even stop texting and driving. Humans often have the capacity to know our habits are toxic, but we don't want to stop. Numbers don't lie—whether that's our weekly spending, alcohol consumption, or screen time reports. That's why using smart, wearable healthcare monitors that track blood pressure, sedentary hours, and sleep could improve our lives.

Big data can also project the consequences of future actions, such as not taking care of your body, leaving too little-to-no mobility in your sixties when you finally have enough capital and flexibility to travel for three months straight. Show a teenage smoker his possible future lungs with chronic obstructive pulmonary disease (COPD) and the joys of breathing out of a hole in his neck if he continues to smoke a pack a day for fifty years. Show a thirty-five-year old what his life could look like depending only on the joke known as social security because he opted out of 401(k) benefits, never created an individual retirement account, and never budgeted for retirement.

Blowing off your wife might be fine once, but a years-entrenched habit will likely lead to an emotionally and financially painful divorce that tech could raise a red flag to years prior. We have the personal freedom to make these decisions if we choose, but sometimes we don't fully comprehend the consequences. Alcoholics Anonymous and Narcotics Anonymous use similar tactics: It highlights real-life, heartbreaking stories of the circumstances through which addiction drags people. By listening to painful decisions like an alcohol addiction so powerful it causes someone to buy booze instead of pay rent, getting your family evicted in winter, or pawning your son's car so you can go smoke crack, you'll understand the dire possible consequences of your actions. Real life is no different. You have to find your "why" to sacrifice, no matter the goal.

Sometimes, we need reminders of what we're supposed to be doing. Sometimes we sleep in past our alarms or our kid called in sick from school so we can't work out. Life rarely seems to slow down as we age. Regular text messages reminding you to go to the dentist, your court hearing, or get a colonoscopy could quite literally save lives by catching life-threatening diseases in the early stages. We can harness tech to accomplish our goals, even when we don't want to. If we leave things unscheduled, we might not even know we missed it. What's measured is managed, as management guru Peter Drucker says (Prusak 2010). Similar to spending all your money before your next paycheck, we should schedule our time priorities, like staying active or studying for the Law School Admissions

Test, or even going on more dates. Scheduling nudges like a reminder to buy new tires before they blowout on the highway or buy groceries or whatever you need keeps us ahead of the game. Preventative "maintenance" is much better in the long run than constantly scrambling to put out fires.

A study called "Behavior Change Implemented in Electronic Lifestyle Activity Monitors" dives into deeper detail of using reminders for exercise and a healthier lifestyle. The study concludes: "Electronic activity monitors include many different empirically tested behavior change techniques that are commonly implemented in clinical interventions. Many of these techniques are associated with successful physical activity and/or weight loss, and implementation of most of the techniques adhered closely to theory-based recommendations."

On the net, technology helps us so much more than it hurts. Oftentimes, men would walk women home to ensure they returned home safely. Pushing drunk girls into a dirty, cash-operated cab wasn't necessarily the best idea—but enter Uber, where the driver and customer are connected by a digital paper trail and a double-ranking system to push out bad actors.

Depending on where you live, it's a coin flip whether you'll get robbed at gunpoint, but SafeTrek, a personal safety app, has garnered over 250,000 users—nearly all of them young women—across the United States. To use SafeTrek, you open it during your walk home, for instance, and keep a finger on the screen's sensor, a process the company calls "hold until safe." Removing your finger triggers a screen asking for a four-digit code. If you enter the code, that's your signal to the app that you've made it home safely—if you don't, SafeTrek calls the police and sends them to where you are. It costs three dollars per month.

Technology has also made incredible services basically free—consider an iPhone, which is a camera, calculator, phone, recording device, from which I can move money in my bank accounts, post on Facebook, or get directions to new places. From 500 miles away, I can Facetime my nephews and family to keep them updated at no additional cost other than the initial purchase and monthly bills from my cell phone provider. Although phones are more expensive than in the early 2000s, they provide so much more utility compared to my first Nokia whose best feature was Snake.

If the COVID-19 outbreak would have happened pre-internet or at least pre-video conferencing and phone software, the world might have stopped. We would have seen food and gas shortages much worse than toilet paper scarcity. Every day, millions of people work to keep the world going. Truck drivers haul goods across the country that are distributed.

Hospitals would have been overrun, grocery stores empty, and there would have been hundreds of millions more deaths than today. And a large portion of that is thanks to technology and science.

For families across the United States, video cameras were the only way to communicate with friends in the hospital and family in nursing homes. A rapid COVID-19 test created only months ago gives a fairly accurate result in fifteen minutes. Investigational monoclonal antibody therapy bamlanivimab and other treatments have saved countless lives, including possibly my father's, and will continue to do so.

If you find yourself unexpectedly hammered at a bar, you can call an Uber and dodge a $10,000 DUI and a possible vehicular homicide charge. While you're spammed with your Amazon search history, they're all items you voluntarily initially showed interest in instead of incorrect demographics, like someone who loves rap being hounded with country music products.

People who live in bad neighborhoods can check out a ruckus using their Ring without stepping outside. Companies can extend a job offer from all over the world through LinkedIn, even if you live between two cornfields in Southern Illinois.

CHAPTER 15

PANDEMIC RESET

COVID-19 CONUNDRUM

When the COVID-19 pandemic struck the United States in March 2020, life drastically changed. The government forced private businesses to shutter, leaving people with few reasons to leave the house. In Michigan, it was illegal to work out in a public gym for months, despite obesity causing a major preexisting condition exacerbating COVID-19's fatality rate (McClallen 2020). So many people gained weight, barely left the house, and spent more time staring at screens for work and play. On a slow day, I would finish my nine-to-five job working in the corner of my apartment, only to continue working in the same corner hours longer on this book. The pandemic and government's accompanying restrictions have overwhelmingly hurt our health. A paper from the US Centers for Disease Control and Prevention found that the portion of five- to eleven-year-olds classified as overweight or obese is now 45.7 percent up from 36.2 percent pre-pandemic.

For some, the pandemic served as a moment of clarity, an opportunity to make life-changing decisions. In August 2021, a record 4.3 million Americans quit their jobs, *USA Today* reported on October 13, 2021.

Some are changing careers. Many love remote work and loathe the idea of a jam-packed, stressful commute only to have coworkers bother them and sit in meaningless meetings, atrophied for hours. Others chose to start a family and live on one income. Everyone still living experienced life or death situations for many elderly or immunocompromised friends, or drastic income changes for business owners who were forcibly shuttered by the government, leaving their workers to hopefully draw unemployment.

We should use this moment to disrupt our online addictions. Moments of clarity often appear when you least expect them—in the shower, hiking in the forest, during break-ups, bankruptcy, or hitting rock bottom. Each one of us can choose our social media rock bottom (maybe you haven't hit it yet). Here are some of mine:

- Facebook outing the sexuality of two college students to the entire world (and disappointed parents) (Fowler 2012).

- Facebook kicking off users for making harmless meme jokes.

- YouTube and TikTok collecting and selling children's data (Kelly 2019).

- The Microsoft-owned search engine Bing censoring the history of the Chinese government's 1989 Tienanmen Square massacre (Campbell 2021).

- YouTube demonetizing popular comedians and show hosts because it disagreed with their beliefs or made funny jokes (in tech's terms, for violating Community Standards) (Alexander 2019).

A "moment of clarity" for alcoholics is when they come to terms with their addiction and how it negatively affects the quality of their relationships, health, and overall well-being. We should have a moment of clarity for social media use by scheduling daily meditation to keep us grounded in what matters rather than what society chooses as its angry take of the day.

My social media moment of clarity hit me like a truck when my phone said I was spending between six and eight hours online daily. Quickly, I assured myself those hours were productive—streaming meetings, press conferences, or sending emails, but numbers and phone-tracking apps don't lie. The sessions I thought were just fifteen minutes stretched to an hour of endless, low-quality scrolling, and instead of work-related apps (Quip, Otter, email, e-books, etc.). My biggest time-wasting culprits were Twitter, Facebook, YouTube, and Reddit. On August 12, 2020, I spent ten hours on my phone—nearly four hours on Twitter, as well as Facebook, although all other single app use was under thirty minutes.

On June 28, 2021, my phone interrupted me 353 times via notifications. Can you imagine if someone followed you for twenty-four hours, tapping your shoulder and screaming every four minutes to do something? Thankfully, that fed me up over a year ago, so I usually place my phone in a box or out of sight when working, while connected via Bluetooth headphones. Using tech has two costs: our exposure and the opportunity cost of doing literally anything else. That's a unique formula for each of us, but I'd encourage you to find it if you haven't already. I've reduced my average online time to two hours and thirty-five minutes per day, (not counting work), harnessing the additional six hours to start accomplishing my dreams—writing this book, reaching reading goals, and getting ripped (work in progress).

Real learning brings fulfillment, while social time-suckers don't in the long run. Too many people lie on their deathbeds with a long, unchecked to-do list. I've set a goal to read forty-four books in 2021 (with notifications to nudge me if I'm falling behind), forcing me to read and learn instead of streaming another disappointing show. I'm at forty-one books.

From the moment we open our eyes to start the day, we reach for our phones, and why wouldn't we?

For one of the first times in history, we can contact someone twenty-four hours a day, seven days a week, 365 days a year across the planet. We can call our mother down the street, or a friend in Hong Kong. This unlimited capacity to be in contact at a moment's notice, regardless of distance, is incredible and terrifying.

Despite these powerful uses, we rely on them to avoid awkward encounters, our AirPods to literally block our potential conversations and street and elevator noises. Then we spend the rest of our day hunched over, staring at either a screen in our hand or front of us. The always-there option to allegedly entertain yourself is strong enough to have shattered most of our attention spans so that we can't read a book for thirty minutes or finish a show or movie without checking our device. Here's a challenge: Sit in silence for twenty minutes with no entertainment. It's uncomfortable, and sometimes can be downright painful. But silencing the constant buzzing of daily life, even just for twenty minutes, can clarify what really matters.

Smartphones are incredibly useful devices, but we've become too reliant on them—often freaking out when we leave a phone, feel phantom vibrations, or try to cure boredom.

For our own good, we should regulate phone and online time so we can focus on real life instead of our online profiles. Our collective online actions have long-lasting effects on society like shorter attention spans and behavioral problems. Our individual actions won't impact general user behavior, but it can change the lives of us and our family.

For example, Harvard research shows regular mindfulness and gratefulness make us happier in the long run. Add in giving to others, volunteering, and in general investing in others, and that's another massive step toward a better life not solely focused on ourselves. The tech world sometimes augments our egos so much we forget that there are more important things like helping others and living life to the fullest. A 2014 study in the UK found phone users checked smartphones 221 times per day—once every 4.3 minutes (Hawley 2021, 75). So, it's not surprising our phones distract us from important work, even if the phone is in the same room or within eyeshot.

"[T]he mere presence of consumers' own smartphones may adversely affect cognitive functioning even when consumers are not consciously attending to them," one study concluded (Hawley 2021, 75).

So, even if a phone is on your desk or on the floor and vibrates, your brain jumps from the task at hand to dozens of possible scenarios including your crush messaging you, someone tagging you in a Facebook status, or maybe your kid got hurt at school. Several apps can likely send push notifications that interrupt your work. So, without even physically touching your phone, the device still wrecks our concentration.

However, we're too addicted to our devices to notice. A 2016 study said we touch our phones 2,617 times per day (Foroo-har 2019, 28). About 79 percent of smartphone users check a device within fifteen minutes of awakening and 33 percent of Americans would rather give up sex than lose their cell phone (ibid.).

Social media and companies post highly charged, emotional topics to drive interactions and use fear and anger to drive readership. Not only does our social media addiction use blunt our day, but it also could screw up our long-term happiness and augment depression, Stanford's Dr. Anna Lembke wrote in *The Wall Street Journal* on August 13, 2021.

"Rising rates of depression and anxiety in wealthy countries like the US may be a result of our brains getting hooked on the neurotransmitter associated with pleasure," Lembke wrote (ibid.).

So, we're being drowned in dopamine hits from Twitter, Insta-gram, streaming services, videogames, and more throughout the day. And once we start, it feels so good we don't want to stop. And pretty soon, it's the only way we get small hits of happiness. We come home from work and wallow in whatever our online addiction. And that makes it harder and harder to ditch your phone since you associate it with downtime and pleasure (mine are Twitter and Reddit).

Lembke explains:

> Not everyone plays videogames, but just about all of us have a digital drug of choice, and it probably involves using a smartphone—the equivalent of the hypodermic needle for a wired generation. Reducing phone use is notoriously difficult because at first, it causes the brain's pleasure-pain balance to tilt to the side of pain, making us feel restless and cranky. But if we can keep it up long enough, the benefits of a healthier dopamine balance are worth it. Our minds are less preoccupied with craving, we are more able to be present in the moment, and life's little unexpected joys are rewarding again (ibid.).

We need to update our expectations of social media and our relationship with phones. But even if we change our behavior, it won't be enough to change the actions of everyone. But small actions can increase our quality of life when it comes to the internet and social media.

Another reason you should ditch or regulate TV news consumption is that it's the most dumbed-down version of the news, especially when it comes to complex topics that need more than a sixty-second soundbite.

Spoon-feed us content—make it so we don't even have to read it or think critically about what we're consuming, one issue Neil Postman warned us about in *Amusing Ourselves to Death*, foreshadowing the consequences of dumbing down complex issues to fit them into primetime television instead of long, written arguments. Instead of reading a 250-page book on energy policy, we watch fifteen-second TikToks or hot Twitter takes or watch thirty-second clips of personalities yelling over each other instead of weighing lengthy arguments.

Currently, TV news gives the most focus—arguably the worst medium for reasoned, logical arguments. Instead of long-forum written arguments, we focus on sixty-second sound bites and people yelling over each other instead of civil debate. The dunk-on-your-enemy environment is best described by former President Donald Trump's politics and Twitter habits, which now might permanently permeate politics.

"I will release my tax returns, against my lawyer's wishes, when she [Hillary Clinton] releases her 33,000 emails that have been deleted," he said during the 2016 debate, which included very little policy substance (Wang 2016).

We've become a nation that picks the issue of the day to be angry about, and some company fundraising plans are simply posting outrageous, sometimes false content for readers so they will immediately donate money, whether that money will be spent well or not. Much material is purposely incendiary, misleading, and fake, designed to spark chaos. And lies can spread ten times faster than truth on social media. The typical political email tells you the "enemy" is doing bad things, so they need you to "rush" thirty-five dollars to stop bad people.

In a world of TikTok and Twitter, a long attention span and the ability to think critically to complete deep work is a superpower. Being able to entertain yourself and others without additional props is as well.

Perhaps as important, we need to eliminate legalese and speak clearly and plainly. We need a reset on the assumption the only role agreeing to the terms and conditions page is the company covering their ass from lawsuits. When speaking at a college in New York, Chief Justice John G. Roberts admitted that he doesn't usually read a website's fine print (Weiss 2017).

It has "the smallest type you can imagine, and you unfold it like a map," he said. "It is a problem," Roberts added, "because the legal system obviously is to blame for that" (ibid.). Providing too much information defeats the purpose of disclosure, since no one reads it, he said. "What the answer is," he said, "I don't know" (ibid.).

Just try scrolling through a terms and conditions page of a website, app, or flight ticket. Those pages are designed to be shrouded in secrecy and are cryptic like attempting to get a media statement from Facebook about why they kicked a page off their platform. When you sign a lease to an apartment, the terms and conditions are relatively plain: Follow these rules, or the landlord has the authority to evict you. The lease states possible consequences of certain actions, and then lets tenants choose their risk tolerance.

Terms and conditions for social media and other privacy concerns should be clear. They say they can sell your data to cops, your insurance provider, or even your employer. The new rule for terms and conditions should be as short as possible and written in layman's terms. Most users have no idea what they have agreed to. That's partly on the user for signing away their data, and partly on the company for writing up a terms and conditions page that's wholly unreadable and hard to understand.

If you speed more than ten miles over the limit, you know the consequences of being pulled over—a ticket, higher insurance cost, detainment, and a possible search—but as far as I know, you're safe from the cop selling your information to an interested third party.

By using social media, you have no idea what the possible consequences of posting are. Your information could be sold, spark an angry column in the *New York Times*, or your preferential vacations spots could be packaged and sold.

Justice Roberts explains in *Riley v. California* opinion on a cellphone tracking case: "These cases require us to decide how the search incident to arrest doctrine applies to modern cell phones, which are now such a pervasive and insistent part of daily life that the proverbial visitor from Mars might conclude they were an important feature of human anatomy."

Once you control your online time, you can do anything with the extra time—drill down on your finances, start lifting weights, cook cleaner, read to your kids, or even start a business. Even if your job requires online time, we can constrain how much time we spend on social media.

Or you might realize social media was an overall time drainer. Social media splinters our time into multiple dimensions: the past, the present, the future, and real life versus virtual life. The problem is that humans are terrible at multitasking, and when we try to do too much simultaneously, we complete nothing.

Modern society uses phones and tech to ensure we're not bored for even five seconds. But your constant Twitter feed can distract you from your kid's first steps; winning your meaningless Facebook comment battle intrigues you more than having late-night, heart-to-heart talks with your wife. Relax. Reach out to people and give them your cell number if they want to truly have a good conversation. Constant interruptions murder deep thoughts and ideas, which have become the norm through news alerts, texts, and other push notifications. We're connected to our phones constantly when we should be doing more productive or enjoyable things. Hard work requires critical thought and energy. If we actually did everything we're capable of, we'd amaze ourselves. Scrolling for four hours drains us and wastes valuable time, which you use as an excuse not to do the things you most deeply want.

Big Tech has a great deal of influence over us, but ultimately, you choose whether they wield that power and how it affects you. You can delete apps and walk away. Instead of entrusting the government to break up Big Tech, we should self-regulate. In reality, the government rarely fixes problems. Just look at United States post-9/11 war spending of eight trillion dollars, according to an analysis by Brown University's Costs of War Project.

Too often, reactionary and misleading online posts garner dangerous behavior. Almost exactly three months after

George Floyd died in the custody of the Minneapolis Police Department on August 27, 2020, the AP/CBS reported a near-riot rocked Lake Street solely because of misinformation spread on social media. Already battered by $500 million worth of riot damages, the Twin Cities were trying to recover (McClallen 2020). Hours after a man was shot to death in broad daylight in Minneapolis' fifty-second homicide of 2020, police closed in on the homicide suspect, who shot himself in the head seconds before police detained him (CBS 2020).

A city still reeling from George Floyd's death, people took to social media to call for "justice" for a Black man whom they claimed was unarmed and shot by police. People gathered, angry, and once again started looting downtown Minneapolis. One man who knew the truth paced the sidewalk and yelled it through a bullhorn, but it was too late: crowds gathered and looted more than fourteen stores, reporters were robbed, and buildings torched as people slept inside, almost burned alive that night, all over disinformation (CBS 2020) (Lancaster 2020).

One problem with social media is how quickly fake news spreads. A brief video only shows one side of the story, and people share the link online, outraged, even though they weren't actually there and only saw a snapshot of what happened. In the Netflix series *Clickbait*, a man named Nick Brewer is kidnapped and beaten. The kidnappers force him to hold signs saying he beat and killed women, and that once the video watch count breaks five million views, the man will die.

But what actually happened was Brewer's dating profile had been hacked; the kidnappers had the wrong man, all because of someone misrepresenting themselves on social media. Especially on social media, things aren't always as they appear.

CLOSER TOGETHER?

Facebook can shoulder you into an echo chamber, but it's imperative you escape and meet people who see the world differently than you and look different than you.

Attempting to quash complex political arguments into sixty-second clips has only divided those who disagree. People regularly forsake family because of each other's political beliefs, something that truly should never happen. We should instead use tech to mend relationships and explain difficult stances. Even Ruth Bader Ginsburg and Anthony Scalia were close friends, whose political beliefs couldn't be more different.

Henry Brechter, the managing editor of Allsides.com, seeks to expose people to information and ideas across the political spectrum so they can better understand the world and each other. One such project starts with the younger generation. Bridge the Divide is getting college kids talking to people who might think differently than they do, talking to people who grew up in different environments—rural, urban—and under different circumstances—single-family households, religious, rich, or poor. Another project, the Red Blue Dictionary, aims to explain terms that mean different things depending on who you are—freedom of speech, fake news, gun control.

Comment sections can be the most toxic places on Earth, but the internet can also facilitate civil dialogue between people who disagree.

"The question is how to get people to want to facilitate civil dialogue on the internet," Brechter said. "Because in a lot of ways, that goes against human nature where we're inclined to seek out these spars and these challenges where we're purely seeking to be proven right or put down someone who might think differently."

The biggest challenges are how do we make it sustainable, and how do we educate people to want to do it, since it's against human nature to listen to arguments you disagree with.

"It's much easier to jump into a comment section on Facebook and go crazy than it is than jump on a video call with a random stranger and have a conversation about a meaningful issue," Brechter said.

One of the great potentials of the internet is that it connects people in a productive, respectful way and ideally advances society and society's best interests. But human nature had other plans. Brechter argued this change must start with education—our parents, our teachers, our leaders. One must understand the other side of an argument to truly understand someone else's views, something we learn in high school debate club.

It's so you can have a proper, productive disagreement. You learn how to argue a point in a well-educated way, even if you disagree with that point, while also learning to respect the other side.

"You need to be able to, at a base level, be able to understand the other side of the argument," Brechter said. "Understand where the person might be coming from, why they might think that way, what experiences in their life have led them to think that."

"Humanizing the conversation allows you to communicate with a level of respect that otherwise would be absent if you hadn't consciously sought out an understanding of their side of the matter. It doesn't mean you have to agree with it or even condone it, but you have to make an effort to see where they're coming from."

Face-to-face or video chat is likely the best platform for civil dialogue.

"If you can see the person, you can see the emotion on their face, you can pick up on body language," Brechter said. "It makes it much, much harder to disrespect someone or to be an asshole when you're looking them in the eye."

Allsides Connect is a mismatching technology platform where you fill out a survey and you're matched with a polar opposite. There are conversation guides to walk you through different topics. This can also be used on a smaller community scale—meet over a beer or a coffee and focus on localized topics.

The world is more complex than we know. I know Democrats and Republicans who each believe the opposite party has "evil" beliefs—that Republicans hate poor people because they oppose raising the minimum wage and that Democrats are immoral because they "want open borders." Neither is true, but political parties and others make too much money pitting Americans against each other. If we really want to understand each other, we should sit down in person, and talk over coffee or beer. It's much easier to rip someone's throat out in an anonymous comment section than when looking them in the eyes.

If we let it, our phones will strangle our life—with tech lords cheering them on because we're using more screen time, meaning more advertising revenue and data to sell. We should unplug regularly from our online communities and focus on the people around us.

CONCLUSION

DON'T PANIC

———

Whether we're swiping our credit card at the liquor store, a license plate reader pings our license plate pulling out of Narcotics Anonymous, or we're surfing the web on an unsecure Wi-Fi connection, the line between public, private, and secret life is now blurred. The government and tech companies are gathering more of our data than ever, destroying the disparity between the public, private, and secret parts of life.

We give power to the government because we trust them to do what is right and not take advantage of that trust. They have a responsibility to protect the information of every user due to the trust we willingly give them. The government's job is to enforce property rights, not fix every bad thing that could possibly happen.

With great power comes great responsibility. As we've seen, it's being abused. I wrote this book because a million tiny tech changes happen concurrently every day, but most of us are too busy with careers, family, and friends to tie the current state of technology together. We must examine these changes and take a good, hard look at how companies are abusing advances in technology that should be used for good. Instead, these entities are using their access to information to spy on the private lives of employees and citizens.

We should remember that social media is a highlight reel, not a look into someone's actual life. If all you do on social media is envy what other people have, then delete it. Comparison is the thief of joy, likely seen in the possible connection between young girls' Instagram addictions that leave them depressed because they don't look like Instagram models.

We should trash legalese and write plain contracts in both everyday life and in terms and conditions, whether that's buying clothes at Target, signing up for Twitter, or adding our fingerprints to a database of the Transportation Security Agency.

My initial theory was confirmed: this topic is insanely complicated. Our entire lives hang in the balance of how this technology is used. We must be aware of the changes occurring and strive to limit the abuse of power that comes with it. In addition to limiting this abuse, we must also seek to maximize the benefits this technology provides.

If Congress tries to revise Section 230, I have no doubt they will screw it up. We should proceed cautiously with changing a law that could derail a service roughly 300 million people in the United States relies on. Many times, the push to "do something" rushes us into poorly made decisions. In this case, it could open many companies to lawsuits that eventually backtracks us to when the internet was a worse product.

Tech giants provide immense good, but they shape our worldview via what's in our news feeds run by vague algorithms, and experiment on us like guinea pigs to spark anger or depression. Social media companies should respect users and provide transparent algorithms.

Initially, tech giants used the internet to create social media with the intention of boosting free speech and providing interconnection between everyday people. As these companies grew and changed, they turned on their users and now use that same power to censor speech they don't like. But we shouldn't panic because we run our lives, not social media companies. Individual action alone likely won't change these companies from censoring and acting hypocritically, but we can't control the entire world. Only mass action and a changing of public opinion toward tech companies can hold them accountable.

This book is meant to get you to think differently about technology and to analyze the motives behind your online feeds. Whether that is being sparked to outrage from a misleading headline, social media recommending you to sketchy groups, or your habit of grabbing your phone the first thing after waking up; I want you to consider all the moving parts.

Social media, video games, and living online exploit dopamine hits that temporarily pleasure our brain. At least, until it runs out and you return looking for the same high that you can't quite reach, much like a heroin addict upping injection dosage chasing a high that person will never reach again, a binge-watcher clicking on "one last episode," or a gamer who needs the perfect final match. We don't need to mandate this reduction, but we should use our own judgment to police ourselves and limit Big Tech's ability to control our actions. There is no one-size-fits-all answer to this. Instead it takes the concentrated effort of the individual. While one person cannot stand up against big tech, if a large number do, they have a shot at toppling Goliath.

We have to find a middle ground so the internet and companies can thrive without continuing the abuse of users.

In the words of technology writer Rana Foroohar in *Don't Be Evil*: "If we can create a framework for fostering innovation and sharing prosperity in a much broader way, while also protecting people from the dark side of digital technologies, then the next few decades could be a golden era of global growth."

As we've seen, the current state of tech is teetering on the edge of falling into tyranny.

We must protect the free and open internet because it's a door to unlimited opportunity for all people. For rural children, it's a gateway to learning about anything they want and a chance to escape the farm (for me, that's literal). For bullied kids who don't fit in and sit alone at lunch, they can escape through books and researching topics that actually matter in their professional careers like finance or construction, or cooking.

Although it's easy to get bogged down in dread and fear of the future, people's goodwill always outweighs the bad. While the rich used to have a clear advantage to access tutors, the internet can provide an equalizer. During the COVID-19 pandemic, students were stuck at home and struggling to learn math, reading, and other topics virtually, sometimes in the same room as siblings trying to learn separate topics and parents attempting to work. But University of Michigan students tutored those struggling kids, giving them personalized help during a confusing time and a global pandemic—even if it meant staying up till all hours of the night (McClallen 2020). The internet equalized education for those willing to grind.

While interviewing over thirty experts for this book, a repeated theme emerged. The internet has created so much more net benefit to society compared to the negatives. Technology is value-neutral; it's the *Wizard of Oz*-like, behind-the-curtain manipulation via vague algorithms, arbitrary censorship, and sketchy selective enforcement of community standards that comprise Big Tech tyranny.

These incredible services are expanding throughout the world like never before. In 2000, there were 360 million people online, Tech Musings says. Twenty-one years later, that number has exploded to 4.8 billion users as of October 2021, according to Datareportal.com.

As internet access expands, it will provide many opportunities for new users. Hand in hand with this is the possibility of exploitation. We have to weigh the policies we set in place now to head off this abuse. Edward Snowden explains how the government has structured laws to allow law enforcement to snoop in your private life. "The law is about making it easier for spies and law enforcement to reach deeper and deeper into your life with a simple warrant stamped by any court," Snowden told Joe Rogan on a podcast.

"We call them public officials and private citizens, but with all of the surveillance, all the data collection, people in power, commercially or governmentally, they know everything about us. And we know nothing about them."

"We break the smallest law, we go to jail, we get a fine, we get screwed, we can't get a job, we can't get a loan. But if they flagrantly abuse their office, their authority, they get a pass."

We must protect the free and open internet before more governments weaponize it, while ensuring people can harness it to build business behemoths like Khan Academy, Amazon, and YouTube, which have likely helped more people than any single government program in history.

Emerging from the COVID-19 pandemic, we must be wary of government continuing the precedent of picking and choosing which private businesses can legally operate, governments creating social credit systems that control our freedom, and which opinions are allowed to be published online.

Governments ranging from China to Egypt have abused "fake news" laws (Economist 2021). As we've seen in China, the government has banned embarrassing topics to them like the Tiananmen Square and Winnie the Pooh. In Egypt, journalist Mohamed Monir spent his dying breaths trying to warn others of COVID-19 after he'd been thrown in jail because he criticized the Egyptian government's response to the pandemic (ibid.). Government must keep its hands off "fake news" laws that will only be abused to cover the government's frequent failures.

These topics don't have clear answers, but this book is a conversation starter to plan our privacy policy for social media and law enforcement surveillance. If we don't have a policy plan, the government will continue to seize our civil liberties and more taxpayer money without providing additional benefits.

ACKNOWLEDGMENTS

———

Thank you to all who read the compilation of my thoughts on this topic over the last decade.

To my family who continually pushes me to do hard things, thank you. Only 2 percent of books started actually reach publication, and now, I know why. I extend my gratitude to my editors from current and past jobs and professors from Hillsdale College and beyond who continually improve my writing.

To Professor Koester: Thank you for DMing me on LinkedIn at nearly midnight in Sept 2020, encouraging me to place my story into the world. At the time, I had no idea he would connect his students to world-famous people including Apple co-founder Steve Wozniak and a co-founder of Netflix Marc Randolph.

Thanks to my apartment mate, Micaiah Rogers, for putting up with me in "book-mode."

To NDP staff: Thank you for making this book a reality and working with me hand-in-hand.

To all of those who contributed to my IndieGoGo Campaign to make this book possible: Erin Williams, Jessica Rawlins, Eveline Hecklinger, Tony Talley, Andrew Wilcox, Jeff Talley, Denton Williams, Daren Wiseley, Patrick Thornton, Nathan McClallen, Deborah McClallen, Robin Williams, Kim Thompson, Eric Koester, Alexandra Negrich, Lisa Teegarden, Julia Zawatsky, Gerald McClallen, Patricia Negrich, Jennifer Hart, Greg Geyman, John Burke, Stevan Bennett, Ema Karakoleva Zawatsky, Mark Englert, Joshua Pincumbe, James Rendleman, Joe Thistleton, Jon Smith, Callista Cody, Micaiah Rogers, Andrew Cureton, Tony Lamb, Maria Hopper, Matt Katz, Adrienne Carrier, Penny Swan, Matthew Grunzweig, Shayna Fields, Kelli Eddie, Jacob Grandstaff, Logan Kauffman, Rachel Solomito, Sam McClallen, Michael McDonald, Jacob Petersen, Christina Mittlestaedt, Dustin Bowers, Tristen Fox, George Ancede, Hayden Ludwig, Crystal Schupbach, Ashley Lane, Jake Kenyon, Ryan Zemel, Frank Bruno, Christian Gajor, Henry Hitt, Kristen Guarino, Venice Lamb, Trey VanAken, Jeffrey Freeberg, Emily Jensen Cummings, Bob Knee, Payton Gill, Mark McClallen, Kyle Huitt, Joe Pappalardo, John Duffy, Nick Talley, Maria Hopper, Ellen Popowitz, Noah Hiser, Everett Ives, Calla Janke, Greg Geyman, Michael Purzycki, Anonymous, Mary Dorroh, Cyndi Talley, Silas Mahner, Alec Yoh, Michael McClallen, Joel Gehrke, Caleb Southerland, Ashley McBride, Matthew Painter, Patricia Nardini, Dorothy Petersen, Andrew Jeschke, Luke Barbrick, Claire Hughes, Adam Stathakis, Josh Lee, Joe Graff, Chris Walsh, Joey Weber, Allison Schuster, Rachel Brewer, Evan Carter, Ian Stodart, Andrew Grayson, Stephanie Short, Rachel Umana, Samuel Leftwich, Anthony Day, Ryan Murphy, Olivia Vaccaro, Sonja Youdes, John Speer, Bert Otto, Michelle Bara, and Brian Christensen.

Your generosity and selflessness during a once-in-a-century global pandemic made this book possible. Thank you from the bottom of my heart. Also, thanks to the contributors who wished to remain anonymous.

APPENDIX

INTRODUCTION

Angwin, Julia. "Dragnet Nation: A Quest for Privacy, Security, and Freedom in a World of Relentless Surveillance." New York: Times Books, 2015.

Gramlich, John. "10 Facts about Americans and Facebook." Pew Research Center. June 1, 2021.
https://www.pewresearch.org/fact-tank/2021/06/01/facts-about-americans-and-facebook/.

Klosowski, Thorin. "The State of Consumer Data Privacy Laws in the US (and Why It Matters)." New York Times. Sept. 6, 2021.
https://www.nytimes.com/wirecutter/blog/state-of-privacy-laws-in-us/.

Perlroth, Nicole. "All 3 Billion Yahoo Accounts Were Affected by 2013 Attack." New York Times. Oct. 3, 2017.
https://www.nytimes.com/2017/10/03/technology/yahoo-hack-3-billion-users.html.

Romano, Aja. "The World Wide Web— Not the Internet—Turns 30 Years Old." Vox.com. March 12, 2019.
https://www.vox.com/2019/3/12/18260709/30th-anniversary-world-wide-web-google-doodle-history.

Saiidi, Uptin, "How Hong Kong Beat Coronavirus and Avoided Lockdown." CNBC. July 2, 2020.
https://www.cnbc.com/2020/07/03/how-hong-kong-beat-coronavirus-and-avoided-lockdown.html.

Welton, Emma. "Gabriel García Márquez in quotes." The Guardian. April 18, 2014.
https://www.theguardian.com/books/2014/apr/18/gabriel-garcia-marquez-in-quotes.

CH. 1

Bigelow, John. "The Works of Benjamin Franklin, Vol. VII Letters and Misc. Writings 1775-1779." New York and London: online version. https://oll.libertyfund.org/quote/benjamin-franklin-on-the-trade-off-between-essential-liberty-and-temporary-safety-1775.

City of Detroit, Michigan's Project Green Light Interactive map. Accessed Sept. 2, 2021. https://detroitmi.gov/webapp/project-green-light-map.

@CrimeADay. "26 USC §5687 & 27 CFR §31.202(a) make it a federal crime to possess a liquor bottle that has been refilled with liquor since it was originally filled." Tweet. Twitter post. Oct. 23, 2020. https://twitter.com/crimeaday/status/1319819138114768896.

Edward Snowden and the ACLU's Jameer Jaffar. "Arguing that you don't care about the right to privacy because you have nothing to hide is no different than saying you don't care about free speech because you have nothing to say. A free press benefits more than just those who read the paper." Reddit Ask Me Anything. May 27, 2009. https://www.reddit.com/r/IAmA/comments/36ru89/just_days_left_to_kill_mass_surveillance_under/crglgh2/.

Electronic Code of Federal Regulations. Section 121.575 https://www.ecfr.gov/cgi-bin/text-idx?SID=b40d2eeb9ebfdfbe6b6f8a90e6e9d10a&mc=true&node=pt14.3.121&rgn=div5#se14.3.121_1575.

Fowler, Jeffrey A. "When the Most Personal Secrets Get Outed on Facebook." *The Wall Street Journal.* Oct. 13, 2012. Accessed Oct. 15, 2021. https://www.wsj.com/articles/SB10000872396390444165804578008740578200224.

Friedrich Dürrenmatt, Traps 23 (Richard & Clara Winston trans., 1960). 15. Posting of Andrew to Concurring Opinions, http://www.concurring opinions.com/archives/2006/05/is_there_a_good.html (Oct. 16, 2006). 16. David H. Flaherty, Visions of Privacy: Past, Present, and Future, in 213

Gorodetski, Isaac and James R. Copland. "Overcriminalizing the Wolverine State: A Primer and Possible Reforms for Michigan." Manhattan Institute. Oct. 28, 2014. https://www.manhattan-institute.org/html/overcriminalizing-wolverine-state-primer-and-possible-reforms-michigan-5724.html.

Granick, Jennifer Stisa. "American Spies: Modern Surveillance, Why You Should Care, and What to Do About It." New York: Cambridge University Press. 2017.

Greenwald, Glenn. TED Talk: "Why Privacy Matters." 3:07. 2014. https://www.ted.com/talks/glenn_greenwald_why_privacy_matters?referrer=playlist-what_your_data_reveals_about_y.

Ha, Anthony. "Edward Snowden's Privacy Tips: 'Get Rid of Dropbox,' Avoid Facebook and Google." *Techcrunch.* Oct. 11, 2014. https://techcrunch.com/2014/10/11/edward-snowden-new-yorker-festival/.

Harding, Xavier. "'Who Cares, I Have Nothing to Hide'—Why the Popular Response to Online Privacy Is So Flawed." Mic. March 22, 2018. https://www.mic.com/articles/188563/who-cares-i-have-nothing-to-hide-why-the-popular-response-to-online-privacy-is-so-flawed.

James, Henry. *The Reverberator*. 1888. https://www.gutenberg.org/files/7529/7529-h/7529-h.htm.

Lord Acton, https://oll.libertyfund.org/quotes/214 (John Emerich Edward Dalberg-Acton, 1st Baron Acton, 13th Marquess of Groppoli, KCVO, DL).

Riggs, Erica. "Mark Zuckerberg Spends $30 Million on Four Homes to Ensure Privacy." *NBC News*. Oct. 11, 2013. https://www.nbcnews.com/businessmain/mark-zuckerberg-spends-30-million-four-homes-ensure-privacy-8c11379396.

Rosenzweig, Paul. "The Over-criminalization of Social and Economic Conduct." The Heritage Foundation. April 17, 2003. https://www.heritage.org/crime-and-justice/report/the-over-criminalization-social-and-economic-conduct#pgfId-1133791.

Solove, Daniel J., "'I've Got Nothing to Hide' and Other Misunderstandings of Privacy." San Diego Law Review, Vol. 44, p. 745, 2007, GWU Law School Public Law Research Paper No. 289, Available at SSRN: https://ssrn.com/abstract=998565.

Vaidhyanathan, Siva. *Anti-social Media: How Facebook Disconnects Us and Undermines Democracy*. New York: Oxford University Press. 2018.

Williams, Trey. "Sharing Netflix and HBO Passwords Is Now a Federal Crime, but Here's Why Not to Worry." Marketwatch. July 13, 2016. https://www.marketwatch.com/story/sharing-netflix-and-hbo-passwords-is-now-a-federal-crime-but-heres-why-not-to-worry-2016-07-12.

CH. 2

Facebook. "Community Standards Enforcement Report Nov. 2019. Guy Rosen. Nov. 13, 2019. https://about.fb.com/news/2019/11/community-standards-enforcement-report-nov-2019/.

Fitzgerald, Michael. "The Court Case That Enabled Today's Toxic Internet." *Wired*. July 8, 2018. https://www.wired.com/story/the-court-case-that-enabled-todays-toxic-internet/.

Holmes, Aaron. " Conservative Outlets Regularly Have the Top Performing Posts on Facebook—but Facebook Says the Full Picture Is More Complicated." *Business Insider*. July 22, 2020. https://www.businessinsider.com/facebook-crowdtangle-data-top-posts-conservative-outlets-2020-7.

H.R. 1978. "Internet Freedom and Family Empowerment Act." Introduced June 30, 1995.
https://www.congress.gov/bill/104th-congress/house-bill/1978.

John Whegemen (@johnwhegeman). "1/6 Some important things to consider about these lists. This isn't a criticism of your analysis, because you're working with accurate engagement data from @Cro." July 20, 2020.
https://twitter.com/johnwhegeman/status/1285358531214888960?lang=en.

Kevin Roose. (@Facebookstop10). "1. Franklin Graham 2. Daily Paws 3. Ben Shapiro 4. Ben Shapiro 5. I Love Paws 6. Ben Shapiro 7. I Love Paws 8. NPR 9. Breitbart 10. Reuters.:" Tweet. Twitter. Oct. 13, 2021.
https://twitter.com/FacebooksTop10/status/1448310727702290436.

Lee, Timothy B. "The Internet's Most Important—and Misunderstood—Law, Explained." Ars Technica. June 10, 2020.

Manjoo, Farhad. "Jurassic Web." Slate.com. Feb. 4, 2009.
https://slate.com/technology/2009/02/the-unrecognizable-internet-of-1996.html.

Masnick, Mike. "As Predicted: Parler Is Banning Users It Doesn't Like." Techdirt. June 29, 2020.
https://www.techdirt.com/articles/20200627/23551144803/as-predicted-parler-is-banning-users-it-doesnt-like.shtml.

Masnick, Mike. "Hello! You've Been Referred Here Because You're Wrong about Section 230 of the Communications Decency Act." Techdirt. June 23, 2020.
https://www.techdirt.com/articles/20200531/23325444617/hello-youve-been-referred-here-because-youre-wrong-about-section-230-communications-decency-act.shtml.

Max Boot (@Maxboot). "Biden needs to reinvigorate the FCC to slow the lies and sedition from Fox and other right-wing broadcasters. Or else the terrorism we saw on Jan. 6 may be only" Tweet. Twitter. Jan. 18, 2021.
https://twitter.com/MaxBoot/status/1351263729904738306.

Morris, Chris. "Meet the 17.9 Million Americans Who Don't Use the Internet." NASDAQ. April 23, 2021. Morris, Chris. "Meet the 17.9 million Americans who don't use the internet. NASDAQ. April 23, 2021.

"National Association for the Advancement of Colored People v. Patterson." *Oyez*, www.oyez.org/cases/1957/91. Accessed 11 Sep. 2021.

NetChoice "About" Page.
https://netchoice.org/about/ Accessed Sept. 16, 2021.

Nicholson, Benedict. "These Were the Top Publishers of Sept. 2020 on Facebook." Newswhip. Oct. 14, 2020. Accessed Sept. 11, 2021.
https://www.newswhip.com/2020/10/these-were-the-top-publishers-of-september-2020-on-facebook/.

Padhi, Catherine. "Ted Cruz vs. Section 230: Misrepresenting the Communications Decency Act." *Lawfare Blog*. April 20, 2018.
https://www.lawfareblog.com/ted-cruz-vs-section-230-misrepresenting-communications-decency-act.

Statista. Joseph Johnson. "Global Digital Population as of January 2021." Sept.10, 2021.
https://www.statista.com/statistics/617136/digital-population-worldwide/.

Statista. "Number of Monthly Active Facebook Users Worldwide as of 2nd Quarter 2021." Sept. 10, 2021.
https://www.statista.com/statistics/264810/number-of-monthly-active-facebook-users-worldwide/#:~:text=How%20many%20users%20does%20Facebook,network%20ever%20to%20do%20so.

Stewart, Emily. "Lawmakers Seem Confused about What Facebook Does—and How to Fix It." *Vox.* April 10, 2018.
https://www.vox.com/policy-and-politics/2018/4/10/17222062/mark-zuckerberg-testimony-graham-facebook-regulations.

Twitter: "Q4 and Fiscal Year 2020 Letter to Shareholders." Feb. 9, 2021.
https://s22.q4cdn.com/826641620/files/doc_financials/2020/q4/FINAL-Q4'20-TWTR-Shareholder-Letter.pdf.

Trump, Donald J. "Donald J. Trump: Why I'm Suing Big Tech." *The Wall Street Journal.* July 8, 2021.
https://www.wsj.com/articles/donald-j-trump-why-im-suing-big-tech-11625761897.

Weissmann, Shoshana. "Jeffrey Toobin Should Be Liable for His Big Reveal, Not Zoom." *Washington Examiner.* Oct. 20, 2020.
https://www.washingtonexaminer.com/opinion/jeffrey-toobin-should-be-liable-for-his-big-reveal-not-zoom.

CH. 3

ACLU. "Surveillance Under the Patriot Act." Accessed Oct. 18, 2021.
https://www.aclu.org/issues/national-security/privacy-and-surveillance/surveillance-under-patriot-act.

ACLU: "Q&A on the Pentagon's Total Information Awareness Program." Accessed Oct. 16, 2021.
https://www.aclu.org/other/qa-pentagons-total-information-awareness-program.

Aratani, Lori. "Secret Use of Census Info Helped Send Japanese-Americans to Internment Camps in WWII." *Washington Post.* April 6, 2018.
https://www.washingtonpost.com/news/retropolis/wp/2018/04/03/secret-use-of-census-info-helped-send-japanese-americans-to-internment-camps-in-wwii/.

Dodd, Vikram and Anushka Asthana. "M15 Opens Inquiry into Missed Warnings over Manchester Terror Threat." *The Guardian.* May 29, 2017.
https://www.theguardian.com/uk-news/2017/may/28/mi5-launches-inquiries-into-failings-on-manchester-arena-bomber-salman-abedi-moss-side-raids-amber-rudd.

Elrick, M.L. "Cops Tap Database to Harass, Intimidate." *Detroit Free Press.* July 31, 2001.
https://web.archive.org/web/20011128034017/http:/www.freep.com/news/mich/lein31_20010731.htm. (This is a wayback machine link. It's not on the active internet).

Gellman, Barton and Sam Adler-Bell. "The Disparate Impact of Surveillance. The Century Foundation. Accessed Oct. 16, 2021. https://tcf.org/content/report/disparate-impact-surveillance/?agreed=1&agreed=1.

Guariglia, Matthew. "Too Much Surveillance Makes Us Less Free. It Also Makes Us Less Safe." *Washington Post*. July 18, 2017. https://www.washingtonpost.com/news/made-by-history/wp/2017/07/18/too-much-surveillance-makes-us-less-free-it-also-makes-us-less-safe/.

Granick, Jennifer. "American Spies: Modern Surveillance, Why You Should Care, and What to Do about It." New York: Cambridge University Press. 2017.

Healy, Gene. "Beware of Total Information Awareness." Cato Institute. Jan. 20, 2003. https://www.cato.org/commentary/beware-total-information-awareness.

Jensen, Joan M."*Army Surveillance in America, 1775-1980*. New Haven and London: Yale University Press. 1991.

Miller, Greg. "CIA Pushed to Add Boston Bomber to Terror Watch List." *Washington Post*. April 24, 2013. Accessed Oct. 16, 2021. https://www.washingtonpost.com/world/national-security/cia-pushed-to-add-boston-bomber-to-terror-watch-list/2013/04/24/cf02b43c-ad10-11e2-a8b9-2a63d75b5459_story.html?itid=lk_inline_manual_2.

Minkel, JR. "Confirmed: The US Census Bureau Gave Up Names of Japanese-Americans in WW II." *Scientific American*. March 30, 2007. https://www.scientificamerican.com/article/confirmed-the-us-census-b/.

National Archives. "Japanese-American Internment During World War II." https://www.archives.gov/education/lessons/japanese-relocation#background.

Neil Richards, "The Puzzle of Brandeis, Privacy, and Speech," *Vanderbilt Law Review* 63, no. 5 (2010): 1295–352.

Olmstead v. United States, 277 US 438 (1928) (Brandeis dissenting opinion).

O'Neil, Tyler. "Australia Debuts 'Orwellian' New App Using Facial Recognition, Geolocation, to Enforce Quarantine." *Fox News*. Sept. 3, 2021. https://www.foxnews.com/world/australia-debuts-new-orwellian-app-using-facial-recognition-geolocation-to-enforce-quarantine.

Salem Media. "How Many People Died in WW1?" History on the Net© 2000-2021. October 13, 2021. https://www.historyonthenet.com/how-many-people-died-in-ww1.

Stanford Encyclopedia. "Martin Luther King, Jr. 'Threats/Attacks against Vietnamese Conflict.'" https://kinginstitute.stanford.edu/encyclopedia/federal-bureau-investigation-fbi.

Risen, James and Eric Lichtblau. "Bus Let's US Spy on Callers Without Courts." *New York Times*. Dec. 16, 2005. https://www.nytimes.com/2005/12/16/politics/bush-lets-us-spy-on-callers-without-courts.html.

W. Samuel Warren and Louis Brandeis, "The Right to Privacy," *Harvard Law Review* 4, no. 5 (1890): 193–220.
https://groups.csail.mit.edu/mac/classes/6.805/articles/privacy/Privacy_brand_warr2.html.

CH. 4

ACLU lawsuit:
https://www.aclupa.org/sites/default/files/field_documents/neill_motion_4-5-10_.pdf.

Ackerman, Spencer and Sam Thielman. "US Intelligence Chief: We Might Use the Internet of Things to Spy on You." *The Guardian.* Feb. 9, 2016.
https://www.theguardian.com/technology/2016/feb/09/internet-of-things-smart-home-devices-government-surveillance-james-clapper.

Allyn, Bobby. "TikTok to Pay $92 Million to Settle Class-Action Suit over 'Theft' of Personal Data." NPR. Feb. 25, 2021.
https://www.npr.org/2021/02/25/971460327/tiktok-to-pay-92-million-to-settle-class-action-suit-over-theft-of-personal-data.

Campbell, Ian. "Microsoft Says Bing's 'Tank Man' Censorship Was Human Error." The Verge. June 4, 2021.
https://www.theverge.com/2021/6/4/22519418/microsoft-bing-china-tank-man-tiananmen-square.

Dupnack, Jessica. "Woman Gets Facebook Timeout for 'Men Are Dumb' Comment, Labeled as 'Hate Speech.'" *Fox News.* July 23, 2021.
https://www.fox2detroit.com/news/woman-gets-facebook-timeout-for-men-are-dumb-comment-labled-as-hate-speech.

Elkind, Elizabeth. "Over Half of Online Recruitment in Active Sex Trafficking Cases Last Year Occurred on Facebook, Report Says." CBS News.com. June 10, 2021.
https://www.cbsnews.com/news/facebook-sex-trafficking-online-recruitment-report/.

Federal Trade Commission press release. Feb. 27, 2019.
https://www.ftc.gov/news-events/press-releases/2019/02/video-social-networking-app-musically-agrees-settle-ftc.

Federal Trade Commission press release. Sept. 4, 2019.
https://www.ftc.gov/news-events/press-releases/2019/09/google-youtube-will-pay-record-170-million-alleged-violations.

Feehs & Currier Wheeler, 2020 Federal Human Trafficking Report, Human Trafficking Institute (2021).
https://www.traffickinginstitute.org/wp-content/uploads/2021/06/2020-Federal-Human-Trafficking-Report-Low-Res.pdf.

Horwitz, Jeff. "Facebook Says Its Rules Apply to All. Company Documents Reveal a Secret Elite That's Exempt." *The Wall Street Journal.* Sept. 13, 2021.
https://www.wsj.com/articles/facebook-files-xcheck-zuckerberg-elite-rules-11631541353.

John Stossel. "The Full Snowden Interview." Dec. 21, 2020.
https://www.youtube.com/watch?v=ZSu4rCizyUM 36:40

Liz O'Sullivan (@lizjosullivan). I'm freaking out about this Amazon Sidewalk mesh
network stuff. Here's why: 1. Amazon is pushing WiFi so you have to send all your
traffic through their access." Tweet. Twitter. Sept. 26, 2019.
https://twitter.com/lizjosullivan/status/1177243350283542528?s=20.

Maayan, Gilad. "The IOT Rundown for 2020: Stats, Risks, and Solutions." Security
Today. Jan. 13, 2020.
https://securitytoday.com/articles/2020/01/13/the-iot-rundown-for-2020.aspx.

Macmillan, Douglas. "Data Brokers Are Selling Your Secrets. How States Are Trying
to Stop Them." Washington Post. June 24, 2019.
https://www.washingtonpost.com/business/2019/06/24/data-brokers-are-getting-
rich-by-selling-your-secrets-how-states-are-trying-stop-them/.

Mitnick, Kevin. The Art of Invisibility: The World's Most Famous Hacker Teaches
You How to Be Safe in the Age of Big Brother and Big Data. New York: Little, Brown
and Company. 2017.

The Video Protection Privacy Act of 1988.
https://epic.org/privacy/vppa/Senate-Report-100-599.pdf.

TikTok's Plaintiff's Motion for Preliminary Approval of Class Action Settlement.
https://www.documentcloud.org/documents/20491862-plaintiffs-motion-for-
preliminary-approval-of-class-action-settlement.

CH. 5

Adam Ford. (@Adam4d). "Really, Facebook??" [posting two screenshots] Tweet.
Twitter. on March 1, 2018.
https://twitter.com/Adam4d/status/969405110324523008.

Biddle, Sam, Paulo Riberio, Tatiana Dias. "Iktok Told Moderators to Suppress Posts
by 'Ugly' People and the Poor to Attract New Users." The Intercept. March 16, 2020.
https://theintercept.com/2020/03/16/tiktok-app-moderators-users-discrimination/.

Conklin, Audrey. "Ex-Google Employee: Big Tech's Biz Model Is 'A Society That Is
Addicted, Outraged, Polarized.'" Fox Business. April 7, 2021.
https://www.foxbusiness.com/technology/ex-google-employee-big-tech-addiction.

Cox, Chelsey. "Fact Check: Satirical Claim That the 9th Circuit Court of Appeals
Overturned Ginsburg's Death." USA Today. Sept. 27, 2020.
https://www.usatoday.com/story/news/factcheck/2020/09/27/fact-check-only-satire-
could-9th-circuit-overturn-ginsburgs-death/3548008001/.

Horwitz, Jeff. "Facebook Says Its Rules Apply to All. Company Documents Reveal a
Secret Elite That's Exempt." The Wall Street Journal. Sept. 13, 2021.
https://www.wsj.com/articles/facebook-files-xcheck-zuckerberg-elite-rules-
11631541353?mod=e2fb.

Isaac, Mike. "For Political Cartoonists, the Irony Was That Facebook Didn't Recognize Irony." *New York Times*. "March 19, 2021. https://www.nytimes.com/2021/03/19/technology/political-cartoonists-facebook-satire-irony.html.

Jarboe, Greg. "VidCon 2015 Haul: Trends, Strategic Insights, Critical Data, and Tactical Advice." Tubular Insights. https://tubularinsights.com/vidcon-2015-strategic-insights-tactical-advice/.

John Stossel. "I get that Facebook faces lots of lawsuits, including ridiculous claims from people with bad agendas. It's hard for Facebook to clean up its site. But I know fa" Facebook post. Sept. 25, 2021. https://www.facebook.com/JohnStossel/posts/419107832910428.

John Stossel. "I hate lawsuits. But last week, I sued Facebook and their 'fact-checker' Climate Feedback. I sued because they LIED in multiple careless 'fact-checks', throttled" Tweet. Twitter. Sept. 28, 2021. https://twitter.com/JohnStossel/status/1442955520541818882.

Krug, Chris. "The Sunday Read: Twitter Blocks Dozens of Legitimate News Stories, and Isn't Saying Why." The Center Square. Dec. 6, 2020. https://www.thecentersquare.com/national/the-sunday-read-twitter-blocks-dozens-of-legitimate-news-stories-and-isnt-saying-why/article_303732e0-363a-11eb-bae5-e7f58cd93d49.html.

Orwell, George. *Animal Farm*. Goodreads. Accessed Oct. 2, 2021. https://www.goodreads.com/topic/show/18208445-all-animals-are-equal-but-some-are-more-equal-than-others.

McClallen, Scott. "Michigan Only Midwest State with COVID-19 Restrictions." The Center Square. June 14, 2021. " https://www.thecentersquare.com/michigan/michigan-only-midwest-state-with-covid-19-restrictions/article_2f90dff8-cd2f-11eb-922c-2334f289352b.html.

Mikkelson, David. "Did CNN Purchase an Industrial-Sized Washing Machine to Spin News?" Snopes.com. March 1, 2018. https://www.snopes.com/fact-check/cnn-washing-machine/.

Moore, Thomas. "Politifact: '60 Minutes' DeSantis Video May Be 'Deceptive Editing.'" *The Hill*. 04/08/21. https://thehill.com/homenews/media/547120-politifact-60-minutes-desantis-video-may-be-deceptive-editing.

Olson, Mark. "Jensen Is Family Physician of the Year." *SWNewsMedia*. May 23, 2016. https://www.swnewsmedia.com/chaska_herald/news/local/jensen-is-family-physician-of-the-year/article_48188beb-c2e3-5cda-8bc2-6926339f5280.html.

Poynter Institute. https://www.poynter.org/ifcn/.

Smith, Cooper. "Facebook Users Are Uploading 350 Million New Photos Each Day." *Business Insider*. Sept. 18, 2013. https://www.businessinsider.com/facebook-350-million-photos-each-day-2013-9.

Spangler, Todd. "John Stossel Sues Facebook Alleging Defamation over Fact-Check Label, Seeks at Least $2 Million." *Variety*. Sept. 23, 2021.
https://variety.com/2021/digital/news/john-stossel-sues-facebook-defamation-fact-check-1235072338/.

Vogels, Emily, Andrew Perrin, and Monica Anderson. "Most Americans Think Social Media Sites Censor Political Viewpoints." Pew Research Center. Aug. 29, 2020.
https://www.pewresearch.org/internet/2020/08/19/most-americans-think-social-media-sites-censor-political-viewpoints/.

Whitehouse, John. "The Data Is Crystal Clear: There Is Absolutely No Evidence of Anti-conservative Bias on Facebook." Media Matter for America. Aug. 20, 2019.
https://www.mediamatters.org/facebook/heres-data-facebooks-bias-report-doesnt-show-you.

Zuboff, Shoshana. "The Age of Surveillance Capitalism: The Fight for a Human Future at the New Frontier of Power." New York. Public Affairs. 2019. online version.
https://archive.org/stream/shoshanazubofftheageofsurveillancecapitalism/Shoshana_Zuboff_The_Age_of_Surveillance_Capitalism_djvu.txt.

CH. 6

Adam Ford (@Adam4d). "Really, Facebook??" [posting two screenshots] Tweet. Twitter. on March 1, 2018.
https://twitter.com/Adam4d/status/969405110324523008.

ADT lawsuit. Filed May 18, 2020.
https://www.courthousenews.com/wp-content/uploads/2020/05/ADTsuit2.pdf.

"Blue Feed, Red Feed: See Liberal Facebook and Conservative Facebook. *The Wall Street Journal*. Aug. 19, 2019.
https://graphics.wsj.com/blue-feed-red-feed/.

Bokhari, Allum. *#Deleted: Big Tech's Battle to Erase the Trump Movement and Steal the Election*. New York City: Center Street. 2020.

Brand-Williams, Oralandar. "FBI Agent at Center of Whitmer Kidnap Probe Assaulted Wife after Swingers' Party, Authorities Say." *Detroit News*. July 21, 2020.
https://www.detroitnews.com/story/news/local/detroit-city/2021/07/21/records-fbi-agent-assaulted-wife-swingers-party-gretchen-whitmer-terror-plot/8041014002/.

Boyd, Danah. "Facebook Must Be Accountable to the Public." Points: Data and Society." May 13, 2016.
https://points.datasociety.net/facebook-must-be-accountable-to-the-public-72a6d1bod32f.

Comparably: YouTube.
https://www.comparably.com/companies/youtube/mission.

Detroit Michigan Project Green Light.
https://detroitmi.gov/webapp/project-green-light-map.

Facebook Investor Relations FAQ page.
https://investor.fb.com/resources/default.aspx#:~:text=Founded%20in%20
2004%2C%20Facebook's%20mission,express%20what%20matters%20to%20them.

Foroohar, Rana. *Don't Be Evil: How Big Tech Betrayed Its Founding Principles and All of Us*. Redfern, New South Wales: Currency 2019.

Galloway, Scott. *Post Corona: From Crisis to Opportunity*. Manhattan: Penguin 2020. p. xviii.

Golding, Bruce. "Twitter Still Holding *The Post*'s Account Hostage over Hunter Biden Leaks." *New York Post*. Oct. 16, 2020.
https://nypost.com/2020/10/16/twitter-still-holding-the-posts-account-hostage-over-hunter-biden-links/.

Hawley, Josh. *The Tyranny of Big Tech*. Washington DC Regnery Publishing 2021.

Hitlin, Paul and Lee Rainie. "Facebook Algorithms and Personal Data." Pew Research Center. "Jan. 16, 2019.
https://www.pewresearch.org/internet/2019/01/16/facebook-algorithms-and-personal-data/.

Jack Dorsey (@jack). "Our communication around our actions on the @nypost article was not great. And blocking URL sharing via tweet or DM with zero context as to why we're blocking:" Tweet. Twitter. Oct. 14, 2020.
https://twitter.com/jack/status/1316528193621327876?ref_
src=twsrc%5Etfw%7Ctwcamp%5Etweetembed%7Ctwterm%5E1316528193621327876%
7Ctwgr%5E%7Ctwcon%5Es1_&ref_url=
https%3A%2F%2Fwww.foxnews.com%2Ftech%2Ftwitter-ceo-jack-dorsey-admits-companys-blocking-of-ny-post-article-was-unacceptable.

Lima, Christiano. "Facebook No Longer Treating 'Man-Made' COVID as a Crackpot Idea." Politico. May 26, 2021.
https://www.politico.com/news/2021/05/26/facebook-ban-covid-man-made-491053.

McClallen, Scott. "Kidnapping Plot or Entrapment? Alleged Extremists Claim FBI Set Them Up." The Center Square. July 22, 2021.
https://www.thecentersquare.com/michigan/kidnapping-plot-or-entrapment-alleged-extremists-claim-fbi-set-them-up/article_44ef3d36-eae4-11eb-b237-e36dfe0854f9.html.

Scheck, Justin, Newley Purnell, and Jeff Horwitz. "Facebook Employees Flag Drug Cartels and Human Traffickers. The Company's Response Is Weak, Documents Show." *The Wall Street Journal*. Sept. 16, 2021.
https://www.wsj.com/articles/facebook-drug-cartels-human-traffickers-response-is-weak-documents-11631812953?mod=article_inline.

Shead, Sam. "Facebook Owns the Four Most Downloaded Apps of the Decade." *BBC News*. Dec. 18, 2019.
https://www.bbc.com/news/technology-50838013.

Shearer, Elisa and Elizabeth Grieco. "Americans Are Weary of the Role Social Media Sites Play in Delivering the News." Pew Research Center. Oct. 2, 2019. https://www.pewresearch.org/journalism/2019/10/02/americans-are-wary-of-the-role-social-media-sites-play-in-delivering-the-news/.

Stern, Joanna. "Social-Media Algorithms Rule How We See the World. Good Luck Trying to Stop Them." The Wall Street Journal. Jan. 17, 2021. https://www.wsj.com/articles/social-media-algorithms-rule-how-we-see-the-world-good-luck-trying-to-stop-them-11610884800.

"The Truth About Algorithms." Cathy O'Neil. RSA. Oct. 17, 2018. 0:25. https://www.youtube.com/watch?v=heQzqX35c9A.

Twitter Company Motto: https://about.twitter.com/en/who-we-are/our-company.

United States Senate Health, Education, Labor and Pension Committee. "For Profit Higher Education: The Failure to Safeguard the Federal Investment and Ensure Student Success." July 30, 2012. https://www.help.senate.gov/imo/media/for_profit_report/PartI.pdf.

Vuocolo, Alex. "Amazon Is Quickly Replacing USPS with Its Own Delivery Network." Cheddar News. Sept. 23, 2020. https://cheddar.com/media/amazon-replacing-usps-with-own-delivery-network.

Wilson, Kirby, Allison Ross. "YouTube Removes Video of DeSantis Coronavirus Roundtable." Tampa Bay Times. April 9, 2021.

Walsh, Joe. "Nigeria Has Banned Twitter—Along with These Other Countries." Forbes. June 5, 2021. https://www.forbes.com/sites/joewalsh/2021/06/05/nigeria-has-banned-twitter---along-with-these-other-countries/?sh=3e354ef1d96c.

CH. 7

Asmelash, Leah. "The Surgeon General Wants Americans to Stop Buying Face Masks." CNN Health. March 2, 2020. https://www.cnn.com/2020/02/29/health/face-masks-coronavirus-surgeon-general-trnd/index.html.

Bhattacharjee, Nivedita. Anuron Mitra, Kannaki Deka, Manas Mishra, Sudarshan Varadhan. "Bodies Float Down Ganges as Nearly 4,000 More Die of COVID in India." Reuters. May 11, 2021. https://www.reuters.com/world/india/indias-seven-day-covid-average-new-high-who-issues-warning-strain-2021-05-11/.

Boyle, Alan. "Amazon to Offer Broadband Access from Orbit with 3,236-Satellite 'Project Kuiper' Constellation." Geekwire. April 4, 2019. https://www.geekwire.com/2019/amazon-project-kuiper-broadband-satellite/.

Center for Tech and Civic Life Press Release. Oct. 13, 2020. https://www.techandciviclife.org/100m/.

Coldewey, Devin. "Twitter Bans James O'Keefe of Project Veritas over Fake Account Policy." *TechCrunch*. April 15, 2021. https://techcrunch.com/2021/04/15/twitter-bans-james-okeefe-of-project-veritas-over-fake-account-policy/.

Conklin, Audrey. "White House, Surgeon General 'Flagging' Facebook Posts for Moderation, Psaki Says." *Fox Business*. July 15. 2021. https://www.foxbusiness.com/technology/biden-flagging-facebook-posts-covid.

Constine, Josh. "Facebook Now Has 2 Billion Monthly Users... And Responsibilities." *TechCrunch*. June 27, 2017. https://techcrunch.com/2017/06/27/facebook-2-billion-users/.

C-SPAN. "President Biden: 'If You Are Fully Vaccinated, You No Longer Need to Wear a Mask.'" May 13, 2021. Video. 0:25 https://www.youtube.com/watch?v=4SkzTa8HRDk.

Deep Singh , Karan and Paul Mozur. "As Outbreak Rages, India Orders Critical Social Media Posts to Be Taken Down." *New York Times*. April 25, 2020. https://www.nytimes.com/2021/04/25/business/india-covid19-twitter-facebook.html.

"Facebook Bans 'Voice of Trump' from Platform." BBC. April 1, 2021. https://www.bbc.com/news/world-us-canada-56598862.

Failory.com's Vine analysis. https://www.failory.com/cemetery/vine.

Foroohar, Rana. "Don't Be Evil: How Big Tech Betrayed Its Founding Principles and All of Us." Redfern, New South Wales: Currency. 2019.

Galloway, Scott. *Post Corona: From Crisis to Opportunity*. Manahattan: Pengiun 2020.

Gov. of India Press Information Bureau. English rendering of PM's address at the World Economic Forum's Davos Dialogue. Jan. 28, 2021. https://web.archive.org/web/20210502062317/ https://pib.gov.in/PressReleseDetail.aspx?PRID=1693019.

Greig, Jonathan. "SpaceX Plan for Global Satellite Internet Service Approved by FCC." *TechRepublic*. March 30, 2018. https://www.techrepublic.com/article/spacex-plan-for-global-satellite-internet-service-approved-by-fcc/.

Halaschak, Zachary. "Taliban Spokesmen Use Twitter to Broadcast Updates on Afghanistan as Trump Remains Banned." Yahoo News. Aug. 16, 2021. https://news.yahoo.com/taliban-spokesmen-twitter-broadcast-updates-161400590.html.

Harris, Mark. "Facebook May Have Secret Plans to Build a Satellite-Based Internet." IEEE Spectrum. May 2. 2018. https://spectrum.ieee.org/facebook-may-have-secret-plans-to-launch-a-internet-satellite.

Hawley, Josh. *The Tyranny of Big Tech*. Washington D.C.: Regnery Publishing 2021.

Herring v. United States Ginsburg dissent.
https://www.law.cornell.edu/supct/html/07-513.ZD.html.

Hern, Alex. "Cambridge Analytica: How Did It Turn Clicks into Votes?" *The Guardian*. May 6, 2018.
https://www.theguardian.com/news/2018/may/06/cambridge-analytica-how-turn-clicks-into-votes-christopher-wylie.

Hillsdale College. "Big Tech and Political Manipulation: Robert Epstein." Nov. 17, 2020. 5:47.
https://www.youtube.com/watch?v=wqtKQgTps_g.

Hiner, Jason and Conner Forrest. "Google Fiber 2.0 Targets the City Where It Will Stage Its Comeback, as AT&T Fiber Prepares to Go Nuclear." Feb. 9, 2017.
https://www.techrepublic.com/article/google-fiber-2-0-targets-the-city-where-it-will-stage-its-comeback-as-at-t-fiber-prepares-to-go/.

Huang, Vicky. "Google Has Acquired 200 Companies since 2001—Here Are Its Biggest Failures." The Street. Jan 12, 2021.
https://www.thestreet.com/opinion/google-s-moonshots-make-crash-landing-13952508.

Hughes, Chris. "It's Time to Break up Facebook." *New York Times*. May 9, 2019.
https://www.nytimes.com/2019/05/09/opinion/sunday/chris-hughes-facebook-zuckerberg.html.

Investors.com editorial. "Funny, When Obama Harvested Facebook Data on Millions of Users to Win in 2012, Everyone Cheered." March 19, 2018.
https://www.investors.com/politics/editorials/facebook-data-scandal-trump-election-obama-2012/.

Jansen, Bart. "Cause of Death Released for 4 of 5 People at Capitol Riot—but Not Officer Brian Sicknick." *USA Today*. April 7, 2021.
https://www.usatoday.com/story/news/politics/2021/04/07/capitol-riot-deaths-cause-death-released-4-5-not-sicknick/7128040002/.

Kanye West, "Power." Kanye West. Aug. 5, 2010.
https://www.youtube.com/watch?v=L53gjP-TtGE.

Klender, Joey. "Tesla (Trsa) Is Worth More than Volkswagen, Toyota, and Honda… Combined." Teslarati. July 13, 2020.

Klippenstein, Ken. "Documents Show Amazon Is Aware Drivers Pee in Bottles and Even Defecate en Route, Despite Company Denial." The Intercept. March 25, 2021.
https://theintercept.com/2021/03/25/amazon-drivers-pee-bottles-union/.

Maas, Jennifer. "YouTube Suspends Right Side Broadcasting Network's Channel Ahead of Trump's Florida Rally." TheWrap. July 3, 2021.
https://www.thewrap.com/trump-rally-livestream-sarasota-florida-rsbn-suspended-youtube-video-right-side-broadcasting-network/.

Maxie, Chasity. "Dr. Fauci Says Vaccinated People Should Wear Masks." WBRC.
July 5, 2021.
https://www.wbrc.com/2021/07/06/dr-fauci-says-vaccinated-people-should-
wear-masks/#:~:text=Fauci%20suggests%20that%20when%20you,Michael%20
Saag%2C%20agrees%20with%20Dr.

Newton, Casey. "Why Vine Died." The Verge. Oct. 28, 2016.
https://www.theverge.com/2016/10/28/13456208/why-vine-died-twitter-shutdown.

Oremus, Will. "Facebook Is the 'Mainstream Media' Now." Onezero.medium.com.
Nov. 7, 2020.
https://onezero.medium.com/facebook-is-the-mainstream-media-now-
f6940f30e34d.

Pew Research Center Mobile Fact Sheet. April 7, 2021. Accessed Oct. 17, 2021.
https://www.pewresearch.org/internet/fact-sheet/mobile/#:~:text=The%20vast%20
majority%20of%20Americans,a%20cellphone%20of%20some%20kind.

Pleasance, Chris. "Gay Men Will Be Crushed to Death by Pushing a Wall onto Them
as Part of Nationwide Return to Sharia Law in Afghanistan under the Taliban, One
of the Islamist Group's Judges Reveals." Daily Mail. July 12, 2021.
https://www.dailymail.co.uk/news/article-9780437/Taliban-judge-says-gays-killed-
toppling-wall-group-takes-Afghanistan.html.

Quittner, Jeremy. "Twitter Announces End Date for Vine." Fortune. Jan. 5, 2017.
https://fortune.com/2017/01/05/twitter-end-date-vine/.

Reklaitis, Vitor. "Facebook, Amazon, and Apple Set Records in Annual Spending on
Lobbying." Marketwatch. Jan. 23, 2020.
https://www.marketwatch.com/story/facebook-amazon-and-apple-set-records-in-
annual-spending-on-lobbying-2020-01-22.

Sankin, Aaron. "What Does Facebook Mean When It Says It Supports "Internet
Regulations." The Markup. Sept. 16, 2021.
https://themarkup.org/ask-the-markup/2021/09/16/what-does-facebook-mean-
when-it-says-it-supports-internet-regulations.

Shearer, Elisa. "More than Eight-In-Ten Americans Get News from Digital Devices."
Pew Research Center. Jan. 12, 2021.
https://www.pewresearch.org/fact-tank/2021/01/12/more-than-eight-in-ten-
americans-get-news-from-digital-devices/.

Soave, Robby. "Perhaps Facebook Supports Section 230 Reform Because It Could
Make Big Tech Even More Powerful." Reason. March 25. 2021.
https://reason.com/2021/03/25/perhaps-facebook-supports-section-230-reform-
because-it-could-make-big-tech-even-more-powerful/.

Statista Research Department. "Facebook's Monthly Active Users." Sept 10, 2021.
Statista.com.
https://www.statista.com/statistics/264810/number-of-monthly-active-facebook-
users-worldwide/#:~:text=How%20many%20users%20does%20Facebook,the%20
biggest%20social%20network%20worldwide.

The Wall Street Journal. "Investigation: How TikTok's Algorithm Figures Out Your Deepest Desires." *The Wall Street Journal.* July 21, 2021.
https://www.wsj.com/video/series/inside-tiktoks-highly-secretive-algorithm/investigation-how-tiktok-algorithm-figures-out-your-deepest-desires/6C0C2040-FF25-4827-8528-2BD6612E3796?mod=hp_lead_pos5.

Twitter. Aftab Alam's account on Apr. 25, 2021.
https://twitter.com/aftabistan/status/1386237271720882177?s=20.

Twitter. Boykin, Keith. May 26, 2021.
https://twitter.com/keithboykin/status/1397543763556380674.

Twitter. Logan Clark. April 9, 2021.
https://twitter.com/loganclarkhall/status/1380632742292033539?lang=en.

Twitter. Thomas Massie. July 15, 2021.
https://twitter.com/RepThomasMassie/status/1415749678604357640.

United States Senate Judiciary Subcommittee. Robert Epstein testimony. June 16, 2019.
https://www.judiciary.senate.gov/imo/media/doc/Epstein%20Testimony.pdf.

Wilson, Kirby and Allison Ross. "YouTube Removes Video of DeSantis Coronavirus Roundtable." *Tampa Bay Times.* April 9, 2021.
https://www.tampabay.com/news/florida-politics/2021/04/09/youtube-removes-video-of-desantis-coronavirus-roundtable/.

Wichowski, Alexis. *The Information Trade: How Big Tech Conquers Countries, Challenges Our Rights, and Transforms Our World.* New York: Harper One. 2020.

CH. 8

Auxier, Brooke, Lee Rainie, Monica Anderson, Andrew Perrin, Kumar Madhu, and Erica Turner. "Americans and Privacy: Concerned, Confused and Feeling Lack of Control over Their Personal Information." Pew Research Center. Nov. 15, 2019.
https://www.pewresearch.org/internet/2019/11/15/americans-and-privacy-concerned-confused-and-feeling-lack-of-control-over-their-personal-information/.

Department of Justice complaint against Derrick Evans. Jan. 8, 2021.
https://www.justice.gov/usao-dc/press-release/file/1351946/download.

Detroit Police Department Project Greenlight.
https://detroitmi.gov/departments/police-department/project-green-light-detroit.

Devries, Jennifer, Natasha Singer, Michael Keller, and Aaron Krolik. "Your Apps Know Where You Were Last Night, and They're Not Keeping It Secret." *New York Times.* Dec. 10, 2018.
https://www.nytimes.com/interactive/2018/12/10/business/location-data-privacy-apps.html.

Eichhorn, Kate. "Why an Internet That Never Forgets Is Especially Bad for Young People." MIT Technology Review. Dec. 27, 2019.
https://www.technologyreview.com/2019/12/27/131123/internet-that-never-forgets-bad-for-young-people-online-permanence/.

General Data Protection Regulation.
https://gdpr.eu/article-17-right-to-be-forgotten/.

Hartocollis, Anemona. "Students Punished for 'Vulgar' Social Media Posts Are
Fighting Back." *New York Times*. Feb. 5, 2021.
https://www.nytimes.com/2021/02/05/us/colleges-social-media-discipline.html.

Hill, Kashmir. "How Target Figured Out a Teen Girl Was Pregnant before Her
Father Did." *Forbes*. Feb. 16, 2012.
https://www.forbes.com/sites/kashmirhill/2012/02/16/how-target-figured-out-a-
teen-girl-was-pregnant-before-her-father-did/?sh=39e9775f6668.

Kerr, Orin. "Use Restrictions and the Future of Surveillance Law." Brookings
Institution. The Future of the Constitution Series. April 19, 2011.
https://www.brookings.edu/research/use-restrictions-and-the-future-of-
surveillance-law/.

Montjoye, Yves-Alexandre de, Cesar A. Hidalgo, Michel Verleysen, and Vincent D.
Blondel. "Unique in the Crowd: The Privacy Bounds of Human Mobility." Scientific
Reports. March 25, 2013.
https://www.nature.com/articles/srep01376.

National Conference of State Legislature report. Barriers to Work: People with
Criminal Records. July 17, 2018.
https://www.ncsl.org/research/labor-and-employment/barriers-to-work-
individuals-with-criminal-records.aspx.

Supreme Court of the United States. *Mahanoy Area School District v. B.L.* Oct. 2020 Term.
https://www.supremecourt.gov/opinions/20pdf/20-255_g3bi.pdf.

Soave, Robby. *Tech Panic: Why We Shouldn't Fear Facebook and the Future*. New
York: Threshhold Editions. 2021. p. 145.

Steinmetz, Katy. "See Obama's 20-Year Evolution on LGBT Rights." *Time Magazine*.
April 10, 2015.
https://time.com/3816952/obama-gay-lesbian-transgender-lgbt-rights/.

Sadilek, Adam and John Krumm. "Far Out: Predicting Long-term Human Mobility."
Microsoft research. Dec. 2016.
https://www.microsoft.com/en-us/research/wp-content/uploads/2016/12/Sadilek-
Krumm_Far-Out_AAAI-2012.pdf.

Scheer, Robert. *They Know Everything about You: How Data-Collecting Corporations
and Snooping Governments Are Destroying Democracy*. New York: Nation Books.
2016. p. preface (x).

Turow, Joseph PhD. "Americans & Online Privacy, The System is Broken."
Annenberg Public Policy Center (June 2003), available at,
http://www.annenbergpublicpolicycenter.org/Downloads/Information_And_
Society/20030701_America_and_Online_Privacy/20030701_online_privacy_report.pdf.

Soltani, Ashkan. Study:
https://ashkansoltani.org/work/knowprivacy-a-web-privacy-investigation/.

University of Rochester Medical Center encyclopedia. Accessed September 7, 2021. Reviewed by Joseph Campellone, MD, and Raymond Kent Turley BSN MSN RN. https://www.urmc.rochester.edu/encyclopedia/content. aspx?ContentTypeID=1&ContentID=3051.

Wakefield, Jane. "Ring Doorbells to Send Live Video to Mississippi Police." *BBC News*. Nov. 5, 2020. https://www.bbc.com/news/technology-54809228.

CH. 9

Bradshaw, Tim and Leo Lewis. "Advertisers Set for a Piece of '*Pokémon Go*' Action." *Financial Times*. July 13, 2016. https://www.ft.com/content/75942b12-48ba-11e6-b387-64ab0a67014c.

Brandom, Russel. "The Regulatory Fights Facing Every Major Tech Company." The Verge. March 3, 2020. https://www.theverge.com/2020/3/3/21152774/big-tech-regulation-antitrust-ftc-facebook-google-amazon-apple-youtube.

Dougherty, Conor. "Jay Edelson, the Class-Action Lawyer Who May Be Tech's Least Friended Man." *New York Times*. April 4, 2015. https://www.nytimes.com/2015/04/05/technology/unpopular-in-silicon-valley.html.

Edelson.com https://edelson.com/inside-the-firm/905-2/ Accessed December 15, 2020.

Federal Trade Commission Press Release. "Google and YouTube Will Pay Record $170 Million for Alleged Violations of Children's Privacy Law." Sept. 4, 2019. https://www.ftc.gov/news-events/press-releases/2019/09/google-youtube-will-pay-record-170-million-alleged-violations.

Feiner, Lauren. "Google Cut Its Lobbying Spending Nearly in Half in 2019, While Facebook Took the Lead." CNBC. Jan. 22, 2020. https://www.cnbc.com/2020/01/22/how-much-google-facebook-amazon-and-apple-spent-on-lobbying-in-2019.html.

Hill, Kashmir. "The Secretive Company That Might End Privacy As We Know It." *New York Times*. Jan. 18, 2020. https://www.nytimes.com/2020/01/18/technology/clearview-privacy-facial-recognition.html.

Hurtibise, Ron. "ADT Employee Spied on Customers for Years through Their Security Cameras, Lawsuit Claims." *South Florida Sun Sentinel*. May 18, 2020. https://www.sun-sentinel.com/business/fl-bz-adt-employee-accused-of-spying-on-customers-20200518-47xspnkjl5eznazekkdyqgmva4-story.html.

Kelly, Makena. "YouTube Calls for 'More Clarity' on the FTC's Child Privacy Rules." The Verge. Dec. 11, 2019. https://www.theverge.com/2019/12/11/21011229/youtube-google-coppa-ftc-creators-videos-childrens-privacy-regulations.

Kelly, Makena. "FTC Hits Facebook with $5 Billion Fine and New Privacy Checks." The Verge. July 24, 2019. https://www.theverge.com/2019/7/24/20707013/ftc-facebook-settlement-data-cambridge-analytica-penalty-privacy-punishment-5-billion.

Kramer, Adam, Jamie Guillory, Jeffrey Hancock. "Experimental Evidence of Massive-Scale Emotional Contagion through Social Networks." Proceedings of the National Academy of Sciences Jun 2014, 111 (24) 8788-8790; DOI: 10.1073/pnas.1320040111.

Liao, Shannon. "Google Reportedly Bought MasterCard Data to Link Online Ads with Offline Purchases." The Verge. Aug. 30, 2018.

Mac, Ryan, Caroline Haskins, Logan McDonald. "Clearview's Facial Recognition Has Been Used by the Justice Department, ICE, Macy's, Walmart, and the NBA." Buzzfeed News. Feb. 27, 2020. https://www.buzzfeednews.com/article/ryanmac/clearview-ai-fbi-ice-global-law-enforcement.

Mac, Ryan, Caroline Haskins, Logan McDonald. "Clearview AI Has Promised to Cancel All Relationships with Private Companies." Buzzfeed News. May 7, 2020. https://www.buzzfeednews.com/article/ryanmac/clearview-ai-no-facial-recognition-private-companies.

Oliveira, Nelson. "Ex-ADT Employee Admits Hacking into 200-Plus Live Cameras, Spying on Naked Woman and Couples Having Sex." New York Daily News. Jan. 21. 2021. https://www.nydailynews.com/news/national/ny-ex-adt-employee-admits-spying-on-customers-naked-women-20210121-kmjkd4qjljhsffxd5uwk6v7csa-story.html.

O'Shea, Dan. "Report: Walmart Developing Facial Recognition Tech." Retaildive. July 9, 2017. https://www.retaildive.com/news/report-walmart-developing-facial-recognition-tech/447478/.

Restubog, Simon, Rajiv Amarnani, Patrick Garcia, Laramie Tolentino, Lemuel Toledano, Robert L. Ting. "Yielding to (Cyber)Temptation: Exploring the Role of Self-Control in the Relationship between Organizational Justice and Cyberloafing Behavior in the Workplace." Journal of Research in Personality. April 2011. https://www.researchgate.net/publication/251505987_Yielding_to_cybertemptation_Exploring_the_buffering_role_of_self-control_in_the_relationship_between_organizational_justice_and_cyberloafing_behavior_in_the_workplace.

Sevilla, Gadjo. "The Best Employee Monitoring Software for 2021." PCmag. Oct. 29, 2020. https://www.pcmag.com/picks/the-best-employee-monitoring-software.

Stern, Joanna. "Department Store Mannequins Are Watching You. No, Really." ABC News. Nov. 26, 2012. https://abcnews.go.com/Technology/department-store-mannequins-watch-eyesee-analyzes-shoppers-webcams/story?id=17813441.

Taleb, Nassim Nicholas. Skin in the Game: Hidden Asymmetries in Daily Life. New York: Random House. 2018. p. 4.

Thomas, David. "Jay Edelson Says Tiktok Settlement, Girardi Bankruptcy Show Class Action Bar Is 'Broken.'" *Reuters*. March 9, 2021.
https://www.reuters.com/article/us-edelson-lawsuits/jay-edelson-says-tiktok-settlement-girardi-bankruptcy-show-class-action-bar-is-broken-idUSKBN2B12SI.

Valinsky, Jordan. "Clearview AI Has Billions of Our Photos. Its Entire Client List Was Just Stolen." *CNN Business*. Feb. 26, 2020.
https://www.theverge.com/2019/7/24/20707013/ftc-facebook-settlement-data-cambridge-analytica-penalty-privacy-punishment-5-billion.

Wessler, Nathan Freed. "We're Taking Clearview AI to Court to End Its Privacy-Destroying Face Surveillance Activities." ACLU.org. May 28, 2020.
https://www.aclu.org/news/privacy-technology/were-taking-clearview-ai-to-court-to-end-its-privacy-destroying-face-surveillance-activities/.

West, Darrell. "How Employers Use Technology to Surveil Employees." Brookings Institute. Jan. 5, 2021.

CH. 10

Biddle, Sam. "Revealed: Facebook's Secret Blacklist of 'Dangerous Individuals and Organizations.'" *The Intercept*. Oct. 12, 2021.
https://theintercept.com/2021/10/12/facebook-secret-blacklist-dangerous/?utm_medium=email&utm_source=The+Intercept+Newsletter.

Coaston, Jane. "YouTube, Facebook, and Apple's Ban on Alex Jones, Explained." Vox.com. Aug. 6, 2018.
https://www.vox.com/2018/8/6/17655658/alex-jones-facebook-youtube-conspiracy-theories.

Dangor, Graison. "CDC's Six-Foot Social Distancing Rule Was 'Arbitrary,' Says Former FDA Commissioner." *Forbes*. Sept. 19, 2021.
https://www.forbes.com/sites/graisondangor/2021/09/19/cdcs-six-foot-social-distancing-rule-was-arbitrary-says-former-fda-commissioner/?sh=4bofffc8e8e6.

Davidson, Helen. "Twitter Removes China US Embassy Post Saying Uighur Women No Longer 'Baby-Making' Machines.'" *The Guardian*. Jan. 10, 2021.
https://www.theguardian.com/world/2021/jan/10/twitter-removes-china-us-embassy-post-saying-uighur-women-no-longer-baby-making-machines.

Devine, Curt. Donie O'Sullivan, Kara Scannell. "Twitter Permanently Suspends Steve Bannon Account after Talk of Beheading." Nov. 6, 2020.
https://www.cnn.com/2020/11/05/tech/steve-bannon-twitter-permanent-suspension/index.html.

Encyclopedia Britannica.com. "Exile law." Geoffrey Abbott. Accessed Sept. 10, 2021.
https://www.britannica.com/topic/exile-law.

Irrera, Anna. "PayPal to Research Transactions That Fund Hate Groups, Extremists." Reuters. July 26, 2021.
https://www.reuters.com/business/finance/paypal-research-blocking-transactions-that-fund-hate-groups-extremists-2021-07-26/.

Laughplanet. "Twitter Is Not a Real Place-Dave Chapelle #Shorts." Oct. 9, 2021. 0:11. https://www.youtube.com/watch?v=kS-E6VtD_rE.

Lima, Cristiano. "Social Media: Where Trump Is Welcome—and Where He's Still Banned." Politico. May 5, 2021. https://www.politico.com/news/2021/05/05/where-trump-can-and-cant-post-on-social-media-facebook-twitter-485343.

Luca, Michael. "Social Media Bans Are Really, Actually, Shockingly Common." *Wired.* Jan. 20, 2021. https://www.wired.com/story/opinion-social-media-bans-are-really-actually-shockingly-common/.

Lukianoff, Greg and Jonathan Haidt. "The Coddling of the American Mind: How Good Intentions and Bad Ideas Are Setting up a Generation for Failure." New York: Penguin Press. 2018. Introduction.

McClallen, Scott. "'Please Allow Us to Work': Operation Gridlock Jams Lansing in Protest of Whitmer's Restrictions." The Center Square. April 15, 2020. https://www.thecentersquare.com/michigan/please-allow-us-to-work-operation-gridlock-jams-lansing-in-protest-of-whitmers-restrictions/article_341df1a6-7f4b-11ea-96e2-771c9b9b2f43.html.

McClallen, Scott. "Facebook Shuts Down Michigan Anti-quarantine Group." The Center Square. May 13, 2020. https://www.thecentersquare.com/michigan/facebook-shuts-down-michigan-anti-quarantine-group/article_1166bf1a-9555-11ea-a64e-376ade8b24e0.html.

Nealing, Steve. "Gov. Whitmer Becomes Target of Dozens of Threats on Private Facebook Groups Ahead of Armed Rally in Lansing." *Detroit Metro Times.* May 11, 2020. https://www.metrotimes.com/news-hits/archives/2020/05/11/whitmer-becomes-target-of-dozens-of-threats-on-private-facebook-groups-ahead-of-armed-rally-in-lansing.

Paul, Kari. "Facebook and Twitter Restrict Controversial *New York Post* Story on Joe Biden." *The Guardian.* Oct. 14, 2020. https://www.theguardian.com/technology/2020/oct/14/facebook-twitter-new-york-post-hunter-biden.

Seligman, Lara. "'Tragic Mistake': Us Determines Kabul Drone Strike Killed Innocent Aid Worker, Nine Family Members." Politico. Sept. 17, 2021. https://www.politico.com/news/2021/09/17/tragic-mistake-us-drone-strike-512586.

Tate, Kristin. "Coming Soon: American's Own Social Credit System." *The Hill.* Aug. 3, 2021. https://thehill.com/opinion/finance/565860-coming-soon-americas-own-social-credit-system.

Twitter: "Permanent suspension of @realdonaltrump." Jan. 8, 2021. https://blog.twitter.com/en_us/topics/company/2020/suspension.

Whittaker, J. The Online Behaviors of Islamic State Terrorists in the United States. *Criminol Public Policy.* 2021; 20: 177–203. https://doi.org/10.1111/1745-9133.12537.

CH. 11

"A Bicycle Tragedy." *New York Times.* June 11, 1880.
https://www.nytimes.com/1880/06/11/archives/a-bicycle-tragedy.html.

Anthony Kalamut. "This Is Your Brain... This Is Your Brain on Drugs–80s
Partnership for a Drug Free America." March 21, 2010.
https://www.youtube.com/watch?v=GOnENVylxPI. 0:21.

Centers for Disease Control and Prevention. "Smoking and Tobacco Use. Fast Facts.
Accessed Oct. 6, 2021.
https://www.cdc.gov/tobacco/data_statistics/fact_sheets/fast_facts/index.
htm#:~:text=Cigarette%20smoking%20is%20responsible%20for,or%201%2C300%20
deaths%20every%20day.&text=On%20average%2C%20smokers%20die%2010%20
years%20earlier%20than%20nonsmokers.

Estes, Adam. "Facebook Is Having a Big Oil Moment." Recode. Oct. 6, 2021.
https://www.vox.com/recode/22712348/facebook-whistleblower-outage-oil.

Haidt, Jonathan and Nick Allen. "Scrutinizing the Effects of Digital Technology on
Mental Health." Nature.com. Feb. 10, 2020.
https://www.nature.com/articles/d41586-020-00296-x?utm_source=twt_nv&utm_
medium=social&utm_campaign=newsandviews.

Horwitz, Jeff, and Deepa Seetharaman. "Facebook Executives Shut Down Efforts To
Make the Site Less Divisive." *The Wall Street Journal.* May 26, 2020.
https://www.wsj.com/articles/facebook-knows-it-encourages-division-top-
executives-nixed-solutions-11590507499.

Jonathan Haidt (@Jonhaidt). "but the change for teen girls is massive, esp. for
pre-teens, for whom the rate has nearly tripled. This also shows that the rise in
depression is NOT just a ch...." Tweet. Twitter. Jan. 9, 2019.
https://twitter.com/jonhaidt/status/1083018993991077888?lang=en.

Mark Zuckerberg. " I wanted to share a note I wrote to everyone at our company.

---Hey everyone: it's been quite a week, and I wanted to share some thoughts with all
of you. First" Facebook post. Oct. 5, 2021.
https://www.facebook.com/zuck/posts/10113961365418581Accessed Oct. 7, 2021.

McClallen, Scott. "Minnesota Sets All-Time Homicide Record in 2020." The Center
Square. July 28, 2021.
https://www.thecentersquare.com/minnesota/minnesota-sets-all-time-homicide-
record-in-2020/article_68df3ce2-efa7-11eb-b749-ffc51ff9a735.html.

Moore, Kasey. "How Long Would It Take to Watch All of Netflix?" What's on
Netflix.com. March 31, 2020.
https://www.whats-on-netflix.com/news/how-long-would-it-take-to-watch-all-of-netflix/.

Oremus, Will. "Who Controls Your Facebook Feed." Slate. Jan. 3, 2016.
http://www.slate.com/articles/technology/cover_story/2016/01/how_facebook_s_
news_feed_algorithm_works.single.html.

O'Neil, Cathy. "Why We Need Accountable Algorithms." Cato Unbound. Aug. 7, 2017. https://www.cato-unbound.org/2017/08/07/cathy-oneil/why-we-need-accountable-algorithms.

Read, Max. "Going Postal: A Psychoanalytic Reading of Social Media and the Death Drive." BookForum. Sept/Oct/Nov 2020 issue. https://www.bookforum.com/print/2703/a-psychoanalytic-reading-of-social-media-and-the-death-drive-24171.

Schull, Natasha. "Machines, Medication, Modulation: Circuits of Dependency and Self-Care in Las Vegas." https://www.natashadowschull.org/wp-content/uploads/2018/05/journalart-Schull-CMP-machines-mediation-modulation-curcuits-of-dependency-vegas.pdf.

Scores Sports Bar Mpls Rebuild. May 28, 2020. GoFundme. https://www.gofundme.com/f/scores-bar-mpls-riot-rebuild.

Sherman, Lauren, Ashley Payton, Leanna Hernandez, Patricia Greenfield, and Mirella Dapretto. "The Power of the Like in Adolescence: Effects of Peer Influence on Neural and Behavioral Responses to Social Media." July 27, 2016. National Library of Medicine. https://pubmed.ncbi.nlm.nih.gov/27247125/.

Solana, Mike. "Bombshell." Oct. 4, 20201. Pirate Wires. Accessed Oct. 7, 2021. https://www.piratewires.com/p/bombshell.

Vaidhyanathan, Siva. *Anti-social Media: How Facebook Disconnects Us and Undermines Democracy.* New York: Oxford Press. 2018.

Wells, Georgia, Jeff Horwitz, and Deepa Seetharaman. "Facebook Knows Instagram Is Toxic for Teen Girls, Company Documents Show." *The Wall Street Journal.* Sept. 14, 2021. https://www.wsj.com/articles/facebook-knows-instagram-is-toxic-for-teen-girls-company-documents-show-11631620739?mod=hp_lead_pos7.

Wise, Alana. "What Sen. Blumenthal's 'Finsta' Flub Says about Congress' Grasp of Big Tech." NPR. Oct. 4, 2021. https://www.npr.org/2021/10/04/1043150167/sen-blumenthals-finsta-flub-renews-questions-about-congress-grasp-of-big-tech.

CH. 12

ACLU Complaint. June 24, 2020. https://cdn.arstechnica.net/wp-content/uploads/2020/06/dpd_complaint_v_final.pdf.

Allyn, Bobby. "The Computer Got it Wrong: How Facial Recognition Led to False Arrest of Black Man." NPR. June 24, 2020.

Amazon Support. https://support.ring.com/hc/en-us/articles/360032492292-Amazon-Sidewalk-Information.

Burke, Melissa. "Michigan Man Wrongfully Accused with Facial Recognition Urges Congress to Act." *Detroit News.* July 13, 2021.
https://www.detroitnews.com/story/news/politics/2021/07/13/house-panel-hear-michigan-man-wrongfully-accused-facial-recognition/7948908002/.

Cato Institute: Blackstone's ratio.
https://www.cato.org/policing-in-america/chapter-4/blackstones-ratio.

Feathers, Todd. "Police Are Telling Shotspotter to Alter Evidence from Gunshot-Detecting AI." *Vice.* July 26, 2021.
https://www.vice.com/en/article/qj8xbq/police-are-telling-shotspotter-to-alter-evidence-from-gunshot-detecting-ai.

Ferguson, Andrew Guthrie. *The Rise of Big Data Policing.* New York: NYU Press. 2017.

Kaplan, Josh. "Predictive Policing and the Long Road to Transparency." *South Side Weekly.* July 12, 2017.
https://southsideweekly.com/predictive-policing-long-road-transparency/.

Klare, Brendan F., Mark J. Burge, Joshua C. Klontz, Richard W. Vorder Bruegge, Anil K. Jain. "Face Recognition Performance: Role of Demographic Information." IEEE Transactions on Information Forensics and Security, Vol. 7, No. 6, Dec. 2012.
https://s3.documentcloud.org/documents/2850196/Face-Recognition-Performance-Role-of-Demographic.pdf.

Ferguson, Andrew Guthrie. "Beyond Data-Driven Policing." *American Scientist.* Nov.-Dec. 2017 issue.

Guariglia, Matthew. "Police Will Pilot a Program to Live-Stream Amazon Ring Cameras." *Electronic Freedom Foundation Blog.* Nov. 3, 2020.
https://www.eff.org/deeplinks/2020/11/police-will-pilot-program-live-stream-amazon-ring-cameras.

Johnson, Richard R. "Estimating the Cost of a Problem Officer." Dolan Consulting Group. 2017.

Herring v. United States, Ginsburg dissent. Accessed Sept. 11, 2021.
https://www.supremecourt.gov/opinions/08pdf/07-513.pdf.

Holmes, Aaron. "Police Are Tapping into Residents' Ring Doorbells and Home Security Cameras to Stream 24/7 Live Video." *Business Insider.* Nov. 11, 2020.
https://www.businessinsider.in/tech/news/police-are-tapping-into-residents-ring-doorbells-and-home-security-cameras-to-stream-24/7-live-video/articleshow/79161303.cms.

McClallen, Scott. "Detroit City Council Greenlights $200,000 Facial Recognition Contract." The Center Square. Sep. 29, 2020.

Shackford, Scott. "Massachusetts Police Test Out Robot Dogs. Is Dystopia on Its Way?" Reason. Nov. 26, 2019.
https://reason.com/2019/11/26/massachusetts-police-test-out-robot-dogs-is-dystopia-on-its-way/.

Tau, Byron. "Treasury Watchdog Warns of Government's Use of Cellphone Data without Warrants." *The Wall Street Journal*. Feb. 22, 2021. https://www.wsj.com/articles/treasury-watchdog-warns-of-governments-use-of-cellphone-data-without-warrants-11614003868.

Tau, Byron, and Michelle Hackman. "Federal Agencies Use Cellphone Location Data for Immigration Enforcement." *The Wall Street Journal*. Feb. 7, 2020. https://www.wsj.com/articles/federal-agencies-use-cellphone-location-data-for-immigration-enforcement-11581078600?mod=article_inline.

Tau, Byron. "IRS Used Cellphone Location Data to Try to Find Suspects." *The Wall Street Journal*. June 19, 2020. https://www.wsj.com/articles/irs-used-cellphone-location-data-to-try-to-find-suspects-11592587815?mod=article_inline.

Tau, Byron. "Homeland Security Watchdog to Probe Department's Use of Phone Location Data." *The Wall Street Journal*. Dec. 2, 2020. https://www.wsj.com/articles/homeland-security-watchdog-to-probe-departments-use-of-phone-location-data-11606910402?mod=article_inline.

Tau, Byron. "Military Intelligence Agency Says It Monitored Us Cellphone Movement without Warrant." *The Wall Street Journal*. Jan 22, 2021. https://www.wsj.com/articles/military-intelligence-agency-says-it-monitored-u-s-cellphone-movements-without-warrant-11611350374.

Tesla.com. https://www.tesla.com/models Accessed Oct. 12, 2021.

Veliz, Carissa. "Privacy Is a Collective Concern." *The New Statesman UK*. Oct. 22, 2019. https://www.newstatesman.com/science-tech/2019/10/privacy-collective-concern.

Worldometer UK population. https://www.worldometers.info/world-population/uk-population/.

CH. 13

Benaich, Nathan and Ian Hogarth. "State of AI 2020." https://www.stateof.ai/2020.

Copley, Michael. "Human Rights Allegations in Xinjiang Could Jeopardize Solar Supply Chain." S&P Global Market Intelligence. Oct. 21. 2020. https://www.spglobal.com/marketintelligence/en/news-insights/latest-news-headlines/human-rights-allegations-in-xinjiang-could-jeopardize-solar-supply-chain-60829945.

Connolly, Kate. "Germans Must Walk Their Dog Twice a Day, New Law Will Say." *The Guardian*. Aug 19, 2020. https://www.theguardian.com/world/2020/aug/19/germans-must-walk-their-dogs-twice-a-day-new-law-will-say.

Deibert, Ronald J. *Reset: Reclaiming the Internet for Civil Society*. Toronto: House of Anansi Press. 2020. pp. 62-63.

Grauer, Yael. "Revealed: Massive Chinese Police Database." *The Intercept*. Jan. 29, 2021. https://theintercept.com/2021/01/29/china-uyghur-muslim-surveillance-police/.

Haas, Benjamin. "China Bans Winnie the Pooh Film after Comparisons to President Xi." *The Guardian*. Aug. 6, 2018. https://www.theguardian.com/world/2018/aug/07/china-bans-winnie-the-pooh-film-to-stop-comparisons-to-president-xi.

Hill, Matthew, David Campanale, and Joel Gunter. "'Their Goal Is to Destroy Everyone' Uighur Camp Detainees Allege Systematic Rape." *BBC News*. Feb. 2, 2021. https://www.bbc.com/news/world-asia-china-55794071.

Ingraham, Nathan. "FBI's Facial Recognition Database Will Contain 52 Million Images by 2015." *The Verge*. April 14, 2014. https://www.theverge.com/2014/4/14/5613928/fbi-facial-recognition-database-will-contain-52-million-images-by-2015.

Interpol Fact Sheet. Accessed Oct. 9, 2021. file:///Users/scottmcclallen/Downloads/FS-04_Facial%20R_Factsheets_EN_2020-03.pdf.

Kobie, Nicole. "The Complicated Truth about China's Social Credit System." *Wired*. July 6, 2019. https://www.wired.co.uk/article/china-social-credit-system-explained.

Maizland, Lindsay. "China's Repression of Uyghurs in Xinjiang." Council on Foreign Relations. March 1, 2021. https://www.cfr.org/backgrounder/chinas-repression-uyghurs-xinjiang.

Milward, James A. "What It's Like to Live in a Surveillance State." *New York Times*. Feb. 3, 2018. https://www.nytimes.com/2018/02/03/opinion/sunday/china-surveillance-state-uighurs.html.

Mozur, Paul and Aaron Krolik. "A Surveillance Net Blankets China's Cities, Giving Police Vast Powers." *New York Times*. Dec. 27, 2019. https://www.nytimes.com/2019/12/17/technology/china-surveillance.html.

Mozur, Paul, Raymond Zhong, Aaron Krolik. "In Coronavirus Fight, China Gives Citizens a Color Code, with Red Flags." *New York Times*. March 1, 2020. https://www.nytimes.com/2020/03/01/business/china-coronavirus-surveillance.html#:~:text=New%20York%20Times-,In%20Coronavirus%20Fight%2C%20China%20Gives%20Citizens%20a%20Color%20Code%2C%20With,precedent%20for%20automated%20social%20control.

Nelson, Steven. "Half of US Adults Are in Police Facial Recognition Networks." *US News*. Oct. 18, 2016. https://www.usnews.com/news/articles/2016-10-18/half-of-us-adults-are-in-police-facial-recognition-networks.

Pollard, Martin. "Even Mask-Wearers Can Be ID'd, China Facial Recognition Firm Says." Reuters. March 9, 2020. https://www.reuters.com/article/us-health-coronavirus-facial-recognition/even-mask-wearers-can-be-idd-china-facial-recognition-firm-says-idUSKBN20W0WL.

Research Report. "Documenting Xinjiang's Detention." Australian Strategic Policy Institute. Sept. 24, 2020. https://xjdp.aspi.org.au/resources/documenting-xinjiangs-detention-system/.

Shackford, Scott. "How Do You Lose Money Dealing Marijuana? Be a Government Agency." Reason. Sept. 16, 2019. https://www.cbc.ca/news/canada/toronto/ontario-cannabis-loss-1.5282994?cmp=rss.

Shaw, Jonathan. "The Watchers." *Harvard Magazine*. Jan-Feb. 2017. https://www.harvardmagazine.com/2017/01/the-watchers.

Shesgreen, Deirdre. "The US Says China Is Committing Genocide against the Uyghurs. Here's Some of the Most Chilling Evidence." *USA Today* April 2, 2021. https://www.usatoday.com/in-depth/news/politics/2021/04/02/is-china-committing-genocide-what-you-need-know-uyghurs/7015211002/.

Stanley, Jay. "There's Nothing Inevitable about Apps That Track Your Every Move." *ACLU Blog*. Dec. 11, 2018. https://www.aclu.org/blog/privacy-technology/location-tracking/theres-nothing-inevitable-about-apps-track-your-every-move.

Srivasrava, Roli and Anuradha Nagaraj. "Privacy Fears as India Hand Stamps Suspected Coronavirus Cases." Reuters. March 20, 2020. https://www.reuters.com/article/us-health-coronavirus-privacy/privacy-fears-as-india-hand-stamps-suspected-coronavirus-cases-idUSKBN21716U.

Sullum, Jacob. "Are You Getting Camera-Ready?" *The Washington Times*. Feb. 18, 2002. https://www.washingtontimes.com/news/2002/feb/18/20020218-035846-2665r/.

Vanderklippe, Nathan. "Chinese Blacklist an Early Glimpse of Sweeping New Social Control." Jan. 3, 2018. https://www.theglobeandmail.com/news/world/chinese-blacklist-an-early-glimpse-of-sweeping-new-social-credit-control/article37493300/.

Vice News. "How China Tracks Everyone." Dec. 23, 2019. Video, 0:17, https://www.youtube.com/watch?v=CLo3e1Pak-Y.

World Population Review. "The 200 Largest Cities in the United States by Population. https://worldpopulationreview.com/us-cities Accessed Oct. 13, 2021.

Xiamen city profile. https://www.hioffer.com/area/detail?id=181 Accessed Oct. 13, 2021.

Xiamen Travel Guide. https://www.travelchinaguide.com/cityguides/fujian/xiamen/ Accessed Oct. 13, 2021.

CH. 14

Amazon.com. Halo Fitness. https://www.amazon.com/Amazon-Halo-Fitness-And-Health-Band/dp/B07QK955LS.

CVS.com
https://www.cvs.com/shop/ellume-covid-19-home-test-digital-results-in-15-
minutes-prodid-431742.

Department of Labor.
https://www.dol.gov/sites/dolgov/files/ebsa/about-ebsa/our-activities/resource-center/
publications/top-10-ways-to-prepare-for-retirement.pdf. Accessed Sept. 29, 2021.

Elon Musk (@elonmusk). "Not connecting Tesla cars to Starlink, as our terminal is much
too big. This is for aircraft, ships, large trucks & RVs." Tweet. Twitter. March 8, 2021.
https://twitter.com/elonmusk/status/1369051431903268865.

Federal Communication Commission Report. April 16, 2021.
https://fcc.report/IBFS/SES-LIC-INTR2021-00934.

Franck, Thomas. "Social Security Trust Funds Now Projected to Run Out of
Money Sooner than Expected Due to COVID, Treasury Says." CNBC. Aug. 31, 2021.
Accessed Sept. 29, 2021. www.cnbc.com/2021/08/31/social-security-trust-funds-set-
to-be-depleted-sooner-than-expected.html.

Folger, Jean. "5 Advantages of Investing in Your 20s." Investopedia. Jan. 10, 2021.
https://www.investopedia.com/financial-edge/0212/5-advantages-to-investing-in-
your-20s.aspx.

Grover, Michael. "What a $400 Emergency Expense Tells Us about the Economy."
Federal Reserve Bank of Minneapolis. June 11, 2021.
https://www.minneapolisfed.org/article/2021/what-a-400-dollar-emergency-
expense-tells-us-about-the-economy.

Houser, Kristin. "SpaceX Targets Moving Vehicles with Starlink Satellite Internet."
Freethink.com March 13, 2021.
https://www.freethink.com/space/starlink-satellite-internet.

Houser, Kristin. "Starlink Satellites Bring Internet to Wildfire-Ravaged State."
Freethink.com. Oct. 1, 2020.
https://www.freethink.com/environment/starlink-satellites.

"Insurers Need to Plug into the Internet of Things—or Risk Falling Behind,"
McKinsey, January 8, 2017,
http://www.mckinsey.com/industries/financial-services/ourinsights/insurers-need-
to-plug-into-the-internet-of-things-or-risk-fallingbehind.

Investopedia Team. "How Did Mass Production Affect the Price of Consumer
Goods?" Updated August 27, 2021. Investopedia.
https://www.investopedia.com/ask/answers/050615/how-did-mass-production-
affect-price-consumer-goods.asp.

Investopedia Team. "Market Failure." Updated April 6, 2020.
https://www.investopedia.com/terms/m/marketfailure.asp#:~:text=What%20is%20
Market%20Failure%3F,rational%20outcomes%20for%20the%20group.

Kiva.org. Accessed Oct. 1, 2021.
https://www.kiva.org/about/how

Kiva.org. Accessed Sept. 30, 2021.
https://www.kiva.org/lend-by-category/shelter

Lyons, Elizabeth, Zakkoyya Lewis, Jennifer Rowland, Brian Mayrsohn. "Behavior Change Techniques Implemented in Electronic Lifestyle Activity Monitors: A Systematic Content Analysis." *Journal of Medical Internet Research*. August 2014.
https://www.researchgate.net/publication/264868232_Behavior_Change_Techniques_Implemented_in_Electronic_Lifestyle_Activity_Monitors_A_Systematic_Content_Analysis.

Noonlight. Accessed Sept. 12, 2021.
https://www.noonlight.com/.

Prusak, Larry. "What Can't Be Measured." *Harvard Business Review*. Oct. 7, 2010.
https://hbr.org/2010/10/what-cant-be-measured.

Purnell, Newley. "The Internet Is Filling Up Because Indians Are Sending Millions of Good Morning! Texts." *The Wall Street Journal*. Jan. 22, 2018. Accessed Sept. 29.
https://www.wsj.com/articles/the-end-of-typing-the-internets-next-billion-users-will-use-video-and-voice-1502116070?mod=article_inline.

Reichel, Chloe. "Nudging Organ Donation in the United States." Harvard Law Today. Nov. 13, 2020.
https://today.law.harvard.edu/nudging-organ-donation-in-the-united-states/.

Salisbury, Ian. "Meet Richard Thaler, the Man Who Just Won the Nobel Prize for Helping You Save for Retirement." *CNN Money*. Oct. 9, 2017.
https://money.com/thaler-nobel-economist-retirement-savings-nudge/.

Roser, Max. "Proof That Life Is Getting Better for Humanity, in 5 Charts." Vox.com. Dec. 23, 2016.
https://www.vox.com/the-big-idea/2016/12/23/14062168/history-global-conditions-charts-life-span-poverty.

Rosoff, Matt. Yahoo News. "The $3 Million iPhone: How Technology Has Raised Our Standards of Living." Dec. 22, 2014.
https://news.yahoo.com/technology-great-equalizer-020201287.html.

Samuel, Alexandra. "As Remote Work Becomes the Norm, Vast New Possibilities Open for Autistic People." *The Wall Street Journal*. March 8, 2021.
https://www.wsj.com/articles/as-remote-work-becomes-the-norm-vast-new-possibilities-open-for-people-with-autism-11615222804.

Sheetz, Michael. "SpaceX Says Its Starlink Satellite Internet Service Now Has over 10,000 Users." CNBC. Feb. 4, 2020.
https://www.cnbc.com/2021/02/04/spacex-starlink-satellite-internet-service-has-over-10000-users.html.

Stepko, Barbara, AARP Newsletter. Feb. 18. 2021.
https://www.aarp.org/health/conditions-treatments/info-2021/low-vision-technology.html.

Thaler, Richard and Cass R. Sunstein. *Nudge: Improving Decisions about Health, Wealth, and Happiness.* New York: Penguin Books. 2008. Introduction.

Thaler, Richard and Shlomo Benzarti. "Save More Tomorrow. Using Behavioral Economics to Increase Employee Saving." *Journal of Political Economy,* 2004, vol. 112, no. 1 pt. 2." The University of Chicago. 2004.
https://www.anderson.ucla.edu/documents/areas/fac/accounting/save_more_tomorrow.pdf.

Wichowski, Alexis. *The Information Trade: How Big Tech Conquers Countries, Challenges Our Rights, and Transforms Our World.* New York: HarperOne. 2020.

CH. 15

Alexander, Julia. "YouTube Looks to Demonetize as Punishment for Major Creators, but It Doesn't Work." The Verge. June 25, 2019.
https://www.theverge.com/2019/6/25/18744246/youtube-demonetization-steven-crowder-patreon-advertising-merch.

Campbell, Ian. "Microsoft Says Bing's 'Tank Man' Censorship Was a Human Error." The Verge. June 4, 2021.
https://www.theverge.com/2021/6/4/22519418/microsoft-bing-china-tank-man-tiananmen-square

CBS/AP staff. "Unrest Hits Minneapolis after Mistaken Reports of Police Shooting Black Man Who Actually Shot Himself." CBS. Aug. 27, 2020.
https://www.cbsnews.com/news/minneapolis-unrest-national-guard-black-man-suicide-misinformation/.

Crawford, Nita C. The U.S. Budgetary Costs of the Post-9/11 Wars." Brown University. Watson Institute of International & Public Affairs. Accessed Oct. 10, 2021.
https://watson.brown.edu/costsofwar/figures/2021/BudgetaryCosts.

Forliti, Amy and Jeff Baenen. "Misinformation, Police Mistrust Stir Unrest in Minneapolis." ABC News. Aug. 28, 2020. "
https://abcnews.go.com/US/wireStory/minneapolis-calm-morning-mans-suicide-sparked-unrest-72651857.

Foroohar, Rana. *Don't Be Evil: How Big Tech Betrayed Its Founding Principles—and All of Us.* New South Wales: Currency. 2019.

Fowler, Geoffrey A. "When the Most Personal Secrets Get Outed on Facebook." *The Wall Street Journal.* Oct. 13, 2012. Accessed Aug. 17, 2020.
http://online.wsj.com/article_email/
SB10000872396390444165804578008740578200224-lMyQjAxMTAyMDEwMjAxODI3Wj.html [Now deleted].

Grantham-Philips, Wyatte. "Record-breaking 4.3 million Americans Quit Their Jobs in August, New Data Show." *USA Today.* Oct. 13, 2021.
https://www.usatoday.com/story/money/2021/10/13/americans-quit-jobs-in-record-numbers/8433917002/.

Harvard. "Giving Thanks Can Make You Happier." Harvard Medical School.
August 14, 2021.
https://www.health.harvard.edu/healthbeat/giving-thanks-can-make-you-happier.

Hawley, Josh. *The Tyranny of Big Tech.* Washington D.C.: Regnery. 2021.

Kelly, Makena. "TikTok's Parent Company Sued for Collecting Data on Kids." The
Verge. Dec. 4, 2019.
https://www.theverge.com/2019/12/4/20995974/bytedance-tiktok-musically-coppa-
childrens-privacy-lawsuit-youtube.

Lancaster, Jordan. "*Daily Caller* Reporter Robbed at Gunpoint during Minneapolis
Riots." *Daily Caller.* Aug. 27, 2020.
https://dailycaller.com/2020/08/27/daily-caller-contributor-robbed-gunpoint-
minneapolis-riots/.

Lange, Samantha J. MPH, Lyudmyla Kimpaniyets PhD, David S. Freedman PhD,
Emily M. Kraus PhD, Renee Porter DNP, Heide M. Blanck PhD, and Alyson B.
Boodman MD. "Longitudinal Trends in Body Mass Index before and during the
COVID-19 Pandemic among Persons Aged 2–19 Years — United States, 2018–2020."
Morbidity and Mortality Weekly Report. September 17, 2021. CDC. 70:1278–1283. DOI:
http://dx.doi.org/10.15585/mmwr.mm7037a3.

Lembke, Anna. "Digital Addictions Are Drowning Us in Dopamine ." *The Wall
Street Journal.* Aug. 13, 2021.
https://www.wsj.com/articles/digital-addictions-are-drowning-us-in-
dopamine-11628861572.

McClallen, Scott. "Appeals Court Orders Most Michigan Gyms Closed." The Center
Square. Jan. 25, 2020.
https://www.thecentersquare.com/michigan/appeals-court-orders-most-michigan-
gyms-closed/article_0c4ec3da-b6ff-11ea-a26f-fb5aaf7047d2.html.

McClallen, Scott. "Gov. Walz Requests Federal Funding after Riots Caused $500
Million in Damage." The Center Square. July 6, 2020.
https://www.thecentersquare.com/minnesota/gov-walz-requests-federal-funding-
after-riots-caused-500-million-in-damage/article_bcf0f4d4-bfaf-11ea-abc6-
b77194d7f388.html.

Postman, Neil. *Amusing Ourselves to Death: Public Discourse in the Age of Show
Business.* New York: Penguin Books. 1985.

Riley v. California. June 25, 2014.
https://www.supremecourt.gov/opinions/13pdf/13-132_8l9c.pdf.

Wang, Christine. "Trump: I Will Release My Tax Returns When Clinton Releases
Deleted Emails." CNBC. Sept. 26, 2016.
https://www.cnbc.com/2016/09/26/trump-i-will-release-my-tax-returns-when-
clinton-releases-deleted-emails.html.

Weiss, Debra. "Chief Justice Roberts Admits He Doesn't Read the Computer Fine Print." *ABA Journal.* Oct. 20, 2017.
https://www.abajournal.com/news/article/chief_justice_roberts_admits_he_doesnt_read_the_computer_fine_print.

CH. 16

Datareportal.com. "Digital Around the World."
https://datareportal.com/global-digital-overview.

Foroohar, Rana. *Don't Be Evil: How Big Tech Betrayed Its Founding Principles—and All of Us.* New South Wales: Currency. 2019.

Internet World Stats 2021.
https://www.internetworldstats.com/stats.htm

McClallen, Scott. "Volunteer Tutors, Online Learning Helps Students During COVID-19 Pandemic." The Center Square. Sept. 1, 2020.
https://www.thecentersquare.com/michigan/volunteer-tutors-online-learning-helps-students-during-covid-19-pandemic/article_0b4f4b92-ec5d-11ea-bbdb-a3bc2caf6b03.html.

The Economist. "Censorious Governments Are Abusing "Fake News" Laws." *The Economist.* Feb. 11, 2021.
https://www.economist.com/international/2021/02/11/censorious-governments-are-abusing-fake-news-laws.

Tech Musings (blog) "The Incredible Growth of the Internet Since 2000." Oct. 22, 2010.
https://www.pingdom.com/blog/incredible-growth-of-the-internet-since-2000/.